SUSANNE DEFOE

SLEEPING
with the Rabbits

SUSANNE DEFOE

SLEEPING
with the Rabbits

MEREO
Cirencester

Mereo Books

1A The Wool Market Dyer Street Cirencester Gloucestershire GL7 2PR
An imprint of Memoirs Publishing www.mereobooks.com

Sleeping with the rabbits: 978-1-86151-803-3

First published in Great Britain in 2017
by Mereo Books, an imprint of Memoirs Publishing

Copyright ©2017

The address for Memoirs Publishing Group Limited can be found at
www.memoirspublishing.com

The Memoirs Publishing Group Ltd Reg. No. 7834348

Cover design and artwork - Ray Lipscombe

The Memoirs Publishing Group supports both The Forest Stewardship Council®
(FSC®) and the PEFC® leading international forest-certification organisations. Our
books carrying both the FSC label and the PEFC® and are printed on FSC®-
certified paper. FSC® is the only forest-certification scheme supported by the
leading environmental organisations including Greenpeace. Our paper procurement
policy can be found at www.memoirspublishing.com/environment

Typeset in 12/18pt Century Schoolbook
by Wiltshire Associates Publisher Services Ltd. Printed and bound in Great Britain
by Printondemand-Worldwide, Peterborough PE2 6XD

In memory of my brother James, my best friend and soulmate – I miss you every day. Also my youngest daughter Catherine, without whose help and endless patience this book would not have been finished. Thank you for putting up with me. This is for you both.

I loved my mum and dad very much and they loved me, and for all the mistakes they made I miss them dearly. This is my story.

CONTENTS

~elle~

INTRODUCTION

~ello~

'Born out of step,' that's what a friend said to me once – 'I think you were born out of step'.

Until then I hadn't thought of myself like that, but I guess it made sense. Looking back on my life, I realise that I didn't really get it. Always struggling to make friends and at the same time not wanting to – crazy! I used to (and still do) look at other people and wonder how the hell they did it, you know, make friends and keep them. I am always in awe of the ones who have managed to have a long and happy marriage or relationship. I have knowledge of only one kind of love, a certain kind of love, and that's the love for my children. I have no idea what it feels like to love another person within an intimate relationship and I envy those who have experienced that.

Memories I kept inside myself for years have now been put to rest by writing this story. Now I can move on, and if I feel that I am out of step at any time I just take five steps backwards and start again.

CHAPTER 1

Family matters

I was born in 1950, when my mum, Ellen, was 21 and my dad, Jim, was 25. We lived as sitting tenants with an old man called George– he had half the house and we had the other half. We had one bedroom and one sitting room, a scullery, no bathroom and an outside loo.

I grew up within a small community of shopkeepers in High Wycombe, we all lived in the same kind of house –no one was better than anyone else. The dry cleaner's was next door, then the paper shop, hairdresser and barber, fish and chip shop, wool shop, bakers, butcher's, grocery store and a petrol station. When I was hungry I used to pop next door for a bag of chips and maybe a doughnut. I loved doughnuts and still do. We used to get sweets every day, so I guess it could have been called a kid's paradise. Mind you I did have to have nine fillings all at once when I was nine, and that was only in the 1950s.

We lived next door to my grandmother and grandfather, who owned a sweet shop and a café over the road, where my mother helped my Nan. I can just remember that café and my Nan cooking all morning; she did all the cooking herself on one cooker for about fifty workmen who came in every day. It was meat and two or three veg dinners and always a pudding, usually served up with custard. It was all homemade and the men loved it. I remember she wore a pinafore-type garment that she wrapped around her and tied at the back and she always looked very hot and tired. I guess she would have been in her fifties then, not a young woman. I have to admire her, as I know I couldn't do it and I'm about the same age now as she was then.

The tables had green chequered clothes and the drinking straws were waxy to the touch and very long and thick, not like straws today. They stood in a tall glass and smelled old and musty. Funny the things you remember.

Later she sold the shop and it was turned into a greengrocer's. I think that was mainly because my granddad had worked in Covent Garden Market for years and knew a lot about fruit and veg. I knew all the other kids whose parents owned shops, so I didn't have to go outside the community to find friends. I was sheltered and protected by my family and friends and was not at all streetwise, which was a real problem as I got older.

My grandparents had come from the East End during the war. They were not liked much to begin with by the locals, but they were there to stay and my Nan lived and worked in that shop until she was 80, along with my mum.

My brother James was born in 1952, and as we grew we were always outside in the backyard making mud pies or climbing onto Dad's sheds, stealing our next door neighbour's prize flowers and hiding them until we got caught. My dad told our neighbour off for shouting at us –he used to fall out regularly with the neighbours over us. I thought my brother was a bit of a wimp, as he always had to be encouraged to do anything a bit naughty and was always saying "I'll tell Mum". I didn't really take a lot of notice, though he was a bit of a mummy's boy.

My dad kept all sorts of animals in our back yard and garden. He bred budgies and had a pigeon loft, rabbits, a greyhound and a chicken coop. We also had a dog called Dusty, a cat called Tibbs and an aquarium with tropical fish indoors. I had two jackdaws that came everywhere with me and used to sit on the handlebars of my little bike. It must have looked like a zoo. Dad had wanted to become a vet. His family was so poor that he was sent to work as soon as he was old enough, but he sure had his animals. My dad would kill a rabbit or chicken sometimes to eat – that doesn't sound much like a vet, but I guess times were hard and money was short.

One of my first memories was of climbing into the rabbit hutch and snuggling down into the straw to sleep. I can remember hearing my mum calling and calling me, but I didn't answer. I just stayed there until they found me. My mum said they had been frantic because we lived on a very busy road, and I was only two and a half and I was missing for almost two hours. She never understood why I hadn't answered her, and I don't know either. She did say I was a very deep child and difficult to understand, not like James, who was an easy, happy child.

They never stopped me from sleeping with the rabbits after that, and they always knew where to find me.

I watched my dad bring a rabbit indoors once, holding it by its feet. It was so long and floppy that he put it into a cupboard and went off outside. I climbed up onto a chair, opened the cupboard and took him out.

This rabbit was my friend and I had spent a lot of time with him in his hutch. I touched him and he felt cold, so I got some of my dolls' clothes and dressed him up. I put a dress and cardigan, booties and a bonnet on him, then put him in my doll's pram, tucked a blanket around him and took him for a walk. I pushed him up and down the back yard and I remember rocking him in the pram and talking to him.

Mum told me later in life that Dad had put the rabbit in the cupboard to keep it out of my way for a few minutes until he was ready to skin it. It had been for dinner that night, and when he saw it had vanished he had asked me about it, but I said I didn't know where it was. My mum found it still in my doll's pram the next day. I can just imagine the screams.

My mum said I was a strange child and I liked anything a bit gruesome to look at. I was always the first out on the main road if a cat had been run over to have a close look at it. I know what I was looking for; I was trying to see what made it work.

Another thing I used to do apparently was eat snails. I peeled them first of course, or I used to collect quite a few and line them up on the ground and jump on them one at a time. You must remember all this happened when I was very young —obviously I wouldn't kill snails for fun now.

I remember when I was about four or five my Dad

packing a small case with my clothes and telling me he was sending me to the naughty girls' home. I must have really pissed him off about something. I was terrified, but we went out of the front door on to the main road and headed to the bus stop. A bus came along before we reached the bus stop and he started pulling me, along saying "hurry up or you'll miss the bus". I didn't know where this naughty girls' home was and I had never been on a bus alone before. I knew he was going to just put me on the bus and leave me. I don't think fear came into it – it was just sheer terror and my legs wouldn't walk, so he dragged me. I remember vividly the feeling of being abandoned and not wanted and helpless inside.

We got up to the bus stop and stood in the queue and I was sobbing and begging him not to leave me. I remember thinking maybe the bus conductor would know where the naughty girl's home was so that I didn't get lost. Then my dad just picked me up and carried me home, and told me that if I played up again he really would send me away. I remember him being upset when he took me back home. That must have been the first time I saw another side to my dad, the cruel side of him that he didn't seem able to control. So it began; I had learnt not to upset him.

My brother and I had dummies. Mine was always tied around my neck, I guess so I wouldn't lose it or maybe just to keep me quiet. We were coming up four and five when my mum decided to take them away. She waited until we went on holiday to Clacton and pretended to have forgotten to bring them. It worked. I remember being so tired that I didn't care if I had my dummy or not. However for years after that I didn't have a doll with fingers, toes nose or anything else that protruded from it, I had sucked and chewed them all off! Still to this day I like to chew rubber.

I was born with very black hair like my dad; my brother had almost white hair like Mum had had when she was young. She grew my hair quite long most of the time and I would not let anyone brush it but my dad, so you can imagine what sort of a state it was in by the time he got home after playing in the yard and with the mud if I got a chance. My mum said I looked like a gypsy child, and my dad said I used to wait outside on the pavement for his work coach to drop him home. He said the other men's children that came to wait for them were so clean and tidy and then there was me with my long black hair mangled up and muddy face and clothes, but I was waiting for him to brush my hair. He never pulled it or hurt me, so I knew he loved me. At night I used to get into bed with Mum and Dad and twist his hair with my fingers all night, and he used to complain the next day because he couldn't comb it for the knots in it. When Dad wasn't around I used to twist my hair (even more knots). I still do.

It must sound as though my mum neglected me, but that certainly wasn't the way it was. She was a nervous wreck, not that I knew it at the time; I thought it was normal to go to the doctor's every other week with my brother, and to have so many clothes on in the winter that I couldn't put my arms flat against my sides, and not letting us eat fish in case we choked on a bone. She was always so busy looking after us and cleaning the house, smelling the food that she had just bought in case it was off, then throwing it away and getting something else. To us it was normal.

Mum had no spare time to play with us much, in fact I don't remember her playing with us at all, but she did read to us sometimes. I don't know what made my mum the way she was. She was such a worrier, maybe it began after my dad contracted polio when we were just babies and all sleeping in the same room as each other. No one knows why we didn't catch it. Mum said Dad had had a headache which just got worse and worse. He became really unwell and had to go to bed. Then his neck became stiff and mum called the doctor, who said it was most likely the flu and to keep him warm and give plenty of fluids. The next day he was worse again and Mum said he was banging his head on the headboard with the pain, so the doctor, a different one, came back and sent for an ambulance and rushed him to Stoke Mandeville Hospital. They never told Mum at first what was wrong; I don't think they knew. Mum said she got her sister, Auntie Maggie, to look after us while she travelled to the hospital, which was quite a bus ride, to see him. That's when they told her he had polio meningitis. He was so ill he had to go in an iron lung for ages and they said he might never walk again. Mum said she remembered sliding down the wall she was standing against at the hospital, it was such shock. Polio in the fifties was a killer, and she was so worried that we would catch it; I was three and James was two.

They told her to go home and boil all the bedding, blankets, sheets, pillows everything that we slept on in the bed and cots. It was January and freezing, and she couldn't do that because she had no washing machine and no way to dry things; all she had was a sink where all the washing was done, an old copper to heat the water and a big old mangle in the back yard. I can imagine what sort of a state she must have been in. Mum told me that if it hadn't have been for her sister, Maggie, she would never have coped. She told my mum to get the coal fire going as big as she could, and brought down all the bedding and held it in front of the fire until it began to scorch, even the pillows, as it was the next best way of killing the germs.

Mum looked to her sister a lot for help and Auntie Maggie never let her down. She was a strong character with a big personality and she didn't seem to be afraid of anything, even putting herself at risk of catching polio herself and having children of her own that depended on her. I loved you Auntie Maggie.

Dad nearly didn't recover. He came home some months later, but he was never really well after that.

My grandfather died in 1955, so I didn't really get to know him, although I have vague memories of him standing just inside the shop door with a roll-up ciggie stuck to his bottom lip while he talked, and of him pouring some of his tea into his saucer for me to drink and sucking my dummy. I wish he could have lived longer. I think my brother and I would have benefited from that. As it was I had my grandmother, who wasn't like a grandmother at all. She had her shop and work is what she did best, so she wasn't your typical Nan who knits you things and takes you on picnics, but she was the only grandparent I knew.

She took me to the pictures once to see a very old film (I can't remember what it was called) and to the Isle of Wight. She loved the island and had a brother there who had a hotel, but I never got to meet him or his family; they were either away or out when she took me, and she had never let them know we were coming.

We didn't use the phone much in those days. We used to head for the one-armed bandits. She had a real addiction to them – you know the sort of thing, go in with a fiver come out with a pound. But I only ever remember winning, not losing. We would travel all the way down there on the train and then the ferry just to stand in an arcade all afternoon and then go home. But she enjoyed it and it was a day out of the shop.

The shop was always the same, open at nine, closed from one to two for dinner then closed at five thirty. Every late morning Nan would go down the road to the fruit and vegetable suppliers. She usually took me to help her carry any special deals back that she could get, like a box of mushrooms or tomatoes. She had a grip like iron and she would grab my hand and hold it so tight on the five-minute walk there that I used to have pins and needles by the time we got there, and it had no colour in it, so as I got older I used to make excuses so that I didn't have to go with her.

My dad and Nan never got along. There was always a lot of tension between them and as my mum worked for Nan she was always trying to please both of them, and they were both very fiery people. It must have been a nightmare for my mum. Mum was very close to her brother and sister – they were lovely people and I was very fond of them both. They were nothing like my mum, who was quite a few years younger than both of them, but looking back at that time I think they kind of looked out for my mum. I had quite a few cousins and we were all very close in those days.

My dad's family wasn't close. They were always falling out with each other, so I never knew them very well. One of my dad's sisters had a son five or six years older than me. He was around for a couple of years, during a time when my dad and his mum were speaking and getting on OK, and that's when I got to know him. Being older than me, he was like a big brother to start with, until he started to do things to me. At first he made it seem like a game, but as time went on he would threaten to tell my Mum if I didn't let him touch me. Although he was only eleven, maybe twelve, and I was five or six it was abuse, and my life after two years of it was never the same again. He stole my childhood, and everything seemed so different after that. Thank god my dad and his sister fell out again and I never saw them again. I never told anyone about it. Only my brother knew, as he made him stand lookout.

Apart from that time my life up until 1960 was for the most part very happy. They were the best days and I long for them sometimes, but everything changes and eventually we moved away from the little old house next to my grandmother's shop. We didn't move far, a mile or so, but it seemed a long way to me. I had left infant school and gone on to middle school and then had to change to another school because of the distance.

I hated it. I was bullied daily, in school and out of it. We had come from a small community and small schools to what was to become a great big sprawling estate with kids that were streetwise and not at all like me. I stood out in the crowd with my blue coat and matching hat that Mum had bought me in London. My brother didn't escape either. He was such a quiet, passive and happy boy, until about six or seven boys got him on the ground and beat the hell out of him when he was nine. After that he changed and got worse every year until he was completely out of control. He was in trouble with the police from the age of twelve and expelled from school at fourteen.

Some of the worst days were at that middle school. I was hit and punched every day by some of the girls. I had always been quiet, but now I had become so withdrawn that I couldn't even look up. I remember one of the boys in my class mimicking me. He put his hands deep into his pockets, hunched his shoulders and looked at the ground and said "This is how she walks", pointing at me while everyone laughed.

I know it sounds crazy but I had no friends at all, for two years. When I got home I just used to stay in. Sometimes I would go out on to the playground at the bottom of our garden. Now and again I got away with it and nobody noticed me, but sometimes one girl in particular would come up to me and push and punch me and pull my hair. I was so scared I didn't even cry out, even though she hurt me so much she left marks on me. She was one of the local bullies at my new school and she lived about six doors away from my house, so she got me at school and at home as well. When she used to see that she had gone far enough, just before reducing me to tears she would stop and stare at me until I walked away with my head down. I just went back indoors and stayed there until the next day at school, when it started all over again. I was so withdrawn and afraid it's a wonder I ever went out. I remember checking out of my bedroom window to see who was out on the playground before I went out. When I saw she wasn't there I used to go out and try and have a swing or go on the slide.

One day after checking the playground out I went out and sat on a swing. There were three older girls there, about fourteen years old I guess. One of them lived down my road and had always smiled at me so I felt safe, but when I got out there and I looked at her and smiled she ignored me and was whispering to her friends. She started to come over to me and got right up to my face, then pulled her hand back so far and slapped my face so hard I fell off the swing.

God, I was so unhappy and so frightened. I think I tried to tell my mum what was happening, but I don't think she took it seriously. I just didn't know what was going on. I had always been so safe in my life and happy; I think I was in shock. I thought about my friends the rabbits I had grown up with, and wished they were still there so that I could just crawl into the straw with them and sleep and be safe again, but I had got too big for that. I was growing up and this was just the start of how life was going to be for me from now on.

I think my dad had always liked a drink, but shortly after we moved he started to drink regularly and my mum hated it. I don't remember exactly when he became dependent on drink, but he did drink every weekend and through the week sometimes although there was never any drink in the house; I think he must have carried it on him.

One time he decorated our dining room. It was near Christmas and Mum had been out and bought some red and green wallpaper with holly on it which she said was festive looking. It was awful in July though and embarrassing. She had forgotten that it would be staring at us all year round, even while you were eating your salad in the summer heat. Anyway Dad decorated the room in a day and night, and wouldn't stop until it was finished. Apparently he had had a bottle of gin in his shirt pocket and he drank this all through the day and night while he wallpapered the dining room. He finished it and it was very nice, but he was on the floor the next morning completely sauced. That was what he did; he would drink in secret and think that nobody would ever know, even if he was completely out of it. Perhaps he thought we thought he was just asleep or something, god knows what went on in his head. I do know occasions like this were never mentioned afterwards, so it was just like it had never happened. Now I realize that my mum could never have confronted him as that would have been real trouble for all of us, so it was all just ignored. He knew how much she hated alcohol, although I never knew why in those early days.

We were close as a family with my aunties and uncles, and Christmas was a good time. Everyone would come around to our house on Christmas night and there was a knees-up. I remember barrels of beer on tap and loads to eat – my mum really did work hard to get it all together. My uncle used to push all the furniture back against the walls to make room for dancing. Nan was there with her friends Sophie and Moss. She dressed in her real fur coat and hat with her fox tails hanging down her back. That fox fur fascinated me, and every chance I got I used to examine it in detail, the mouth, teeth, whiskers, ears, feet, claws, two tails – it was kind of split in half with the two tails hanging down the front of Nan with two legs and feet, while the head and the two other legs and feet hung down her back. She kept it in a cupboard in her house and I used to play with it quite a lot. The fox's nose held a kind of fascination for me, the nostrils in particular. I used to poke things up them and really try to see inside them; maybe I thought I might find a brain or something. The nostrils became a bit distorted after some years of this abuse and it looked more like a snout in the end, but Nan never noticed. Mum couldn't stand it and was always telling me to "put that bloody thing away". I never knew what happened to the poor fox in the end. I suspect Mum threw it away when my nan eventually went to live with her.

I remember Moss in a long coat almost to the floor. He looked a bit like Alfred Hitchcock but he played the accordion, and when he played the similarity ended. Sophie, his wife, was dressed in real fur with lots of jewellery. They weren't related to us, but they were Nan's best friends so they always came along. Nan sang quite loud and it was all the old knees up songs I think there was a record player. I do remember *Let's Twist Again* by Chubby Checker being played. I was ten and it was the only time we got away with making a noise and just being normal.

These Christmas parties used to go on till the early hours. My brother and I and younger cousins all used to go up on to Mum and Dad's bed, which was covered with coats, and sleep, maybe four five or six of us, until we were taken home. My brother and I always had really nice presents for Christmas; we usually got what we had asked for even though times were hard as far as money went. Mum and Dad both worked, but I never remember going without. Mum hid our presents in her wardrobe once, which she could lock with a key, but it didn't take my brother long to work out where they were. You could see into the wardrobe if you looked through the keyhole and I could see a doll and other things that mum had not wrapped up yet. That was enough for me as I didn't really want to know what we were getting for Christmas, but my brother could never wait, he wanted to see them all now, so he tried to prize the lock open with a screwdriver. He couldn't do it, but that didn't stop him from trying every day to get the door open.

Mum noticed the deep gouges in the wardrobe door and the bent keyhole and asked who had been messing with it. I didn't even stop to think about it, I just said "It's him, he's been trying to get into it since Saturday" – I had no loyalty. His ears went bright red, as they always did when he was caught out or if he tried to lie, so Mum knew it was him. She was so cross, because of the damage he had done to her wardrobe more than anything else.

Anyway that night when we were in bed and Mum and Dad thought we were asleep, Dad tried to open the wardrobe door with a key that would no longer fit. You would think that would annoy him and make him angry, but it didn't. I think he found it amusing. You never knew where you were with him; you just couldn't tell how he would react.

The next day the presents were gone from the wardrobe, but I found them at my Nan's house upstairs in a cupboard. I never told James because I knew he wouldn't be able to control himself – he would just have to look.

Later Mum told me that they were so hard up for money at times they had to go without lots of other things to pay the mortgage. But by working in Nan's shop she always managed to bring home dinner. We kids were never aware of how hard it must have been sometimes. My dad had a good job and must have earned quite good money, but it couldn't have been enough. He couldn't cope with owing money and I know that they did borrow from time to time, so I guess that's when the drinking became worse, that and the fact that he hated where we lived, because they had built so many houses around us where there used to be only fields. He said that when he came home from work at night and turned into our road he felt a black cloud come over his head. He also didn't cope with us growing up.

I don't know when I first became frightened of my dad. All I know is that I stayed afraid of him for the rest of my life.

Dad went onto do shift work, two weeks of nights and two weeks of days, and it was hell at home. When he was on night work we crept around the house until he got up, as any noise would have resulted in us being shouted at and threatened with a good hiding. When he was on days we were quiet when he came home as he did not allow any shouting, screaming, loud laughing or generally anything or else, so we went out most of the time. My poor mum's nerves must have been frayed. We used to play her up because we knew we could get away with it. When she said she would tell Dad, we knew she wouldn't because she knew how he would handle it, so she had no one to help her with us and we became more and more out of control, though my Dad was never told about any of it.

When my brother was about twelve he was getting up at three or four in the morning to deliver bread in a lorry with some delivery driver. He was caught, but I don't think Dad was told for quite a while and by then it had all calmed down. He was expelled from school because of continued truancy. For months he wouldn't stay at school even if he was taken. Again my Dad was not told about this until he was about to be expelled and even then I think he was just told he was going to another school because it would be better for him. Dad just seemed to have no interest in us, and just seemed to give up on both of us. He called us as half-wits. You couldn't talk to him, dared not talk to him, and dared not even look at him. The worst time was Sundays when he had been to the pub at lunchtime. Mum used to always do a roast and it should have been a happy day, all together for that one day, but he was always drunk and the four of us would sit around the table in deadly silence, not daring to say anything. We had learned to look down and pretend to be invisible when he was in drink, as it was easier that way.

He drank more than ever now and my Mum was even more afraid of him. There she was waiting in the kitchen for him when he got home, kettle ready so he wouldn't have to wait until it boiled. She would make sure she stirred the tea for him or he would make a face and get her to stir it for him while he held the cup. He never hit my mum as far as I know, but he did threaten to wrap the kettle round her head once. I wondered how he was going to be able to do that, given the shape of a kettle, and what he would do for his next cup of tea. That was the only time I ever shouted at him. I screamed "Leave her alone, don't you touch her!" I knew I was risking it, but my Mum was my protector and I loved her so much. I was at the top of the stairs and he swung round to look up at me and started to charge up the stairs to get me, so I locked myself in the bathroom. Mum was screaming, and my heart was banging so loud it hurt, with him shouting and banging on the bathroom door "come out of there or I'll kill you!" I don't know what happened then, he must have calmed down, but I do know I wished he was dead so that I could just have my mum all to myself and we would be happy.

There were still times when my dad was approachable, like when he grew his chrysanthemums and used to get me to sit and turn the petals all in one direction ready for showing in the flower shows. It was always summer time and it was a nice time at home. He won quite a few first and second prizes at the shows; he was good at most things he did and he didn't like to lose.

Our back garden was not a place to play in. He put a concrete path all the way around the outside of the lawn and that's what you had to walk on. It didn't take long for us to wear a path straight through the middle of the lawn, but we never got caught. By the time we did he had given up trying to keep his garden so formal, although there was still his huge great prized chrysanthemums with paper bags over their heads to keep off whatever he was trying to keep off them, so we never actually got to see them in the garden as flowers, just brown paper bags blowing in the wind.

In September off we would all go to the local show in town that came every year and he would show his flowers, and he would nearly always win. My brother and I used to eat toffee apples and watch the cattle shows and dog shows, and it always seemed sunny. That really was a good time for me.

One of the presents my brother got for his eleventh birthday was an air gun from which he shot pellets. He used to line his toy soldiers up outside by the fence and shoot them over again and again. He even let me have a go, and I really enjoyed it. We used to spend time alone in the house while my mum and dad worked on Saturdays, and needless to say James took advantage of this. My mum used to hang her washing out before she went to work and one day he used it for target practice – he could be a right sod sometimes. I could hear the gun keep going 'bang' but thought nothing of it. When Mum came home she went to get the washing in and I heard her scream "JAMES!" Of course he wasn't at home by then. I went to see what had happened and Mum said, "I haven't got a single thing without a hole in it!" I thought it was funny until she showed me my knickers. Every pair had a hole, and I had to wear them like that for weeks until I got new ones.

It was dark when James came home, creeping in through the back door and making his way upstairs just in case Mum had told Dad, which she hadn't because she never did. I was so angry with him, I mean I was coming up thirteen and it really wasn't funny at the time as the thought of PE and getting changed with holey knickers was unbearable. I knew Mum didn't have the money for new ones and I just wanted to choke him. None of his clothes had holes in, strange that!

CHAPTER 2

Growing up

I was very much aware that I was quite a lot more developed than some of my school friends and I started my periods just before my 12th birthday. I didn't know what they were. It was towards the end of September and I had been out playing; I was still very immature in lots of ways. I had met a girl who lived down the road from me, my first real friend since our move. We had been on the swings in the park outside. I remember this so clearly because of the impact that day had on me. We both went home as it was getting dark and I went upstairs to change for bed. I left my clothes on the bathroom floor as we always did, and then I went down to watch TV. Sometime later my Mum came into the room holding my knickers and said to me "what have you been doing?" I was mortified. I didn't know what she meant, and then I saw the blood and thought I was ill. I couldn't speak. She just said "Come upstairs with me". She showed me what I had to do and told me this would happen every month and added "you know what can happen now if you go with boys, don't you?" I just nodded yes, but I didn't know.

I don't know why my Mum was so nasty to me. She made me feel as if I had done something terrible, and I have never got over it. I always felt dirty for having periods and she never asked me how I was with them, even though I used to get awful pains and vomiting most months. It was like when she took me to the doctor's when I was almost thirteen. I had whooping cough and the doctor wanted to listen to my chest, so he asked me to lift my bra out of the way. I looked at my Mum and she looked horrified, and said "she hasn't got one on". No, I didn't have one on, did I Mum? I had a vest on, not a pretty vest with lace around the neck and sleeves, just one of those little cherub wool things with short sleeves that you used to put babies in. God, I nearly died of embarrassment again.

The doctor knew me and my family very well, as he had seen me almost weekly since I had been born, and he always said "Aha!" when we came in, and smiled at me. But even he seemed lost for words now. He coughed and said, "Just hold your vest up at the back Susan, while I listen to your chest". That was it; I had asked her about not wearing the sodding vest, although I didn't swear at her. I got home, took the vest off and never wore one again. I had been the only one at school with a vest on and I was sick of it, life was bad enough as it was for god's sake.

Of course this sent her into a panic. I was just getting over whooping cough, it was March, it was cold, and now I didn't have a vest on either so that meant I would probably die soon. I didn't die though, and she reluctantly took me to buy a bra. Honestly, you would have thought we were going to buy something really disgusting like *Lady Chatterley's Lover* which they tried to ban. I only know about the book by the way because my friend's dad had a paperback copy hidden under his bed and she found it and read parts of it out loud to me, and that's about as bad as it gets, wild child that I was.

Anyway, I got the BRA. Next came putting it on, not easy when you've never put one on before. It must have taken about an hour of adjusting it to get it just right, so much more complicated than the vest. Had I done the right thing? In the end I did the hooks up and just stepped into it like a skirt and pulled it up to where it had to go around my chest. Then I was conscious of it. I thought you could see it through my clothes, so I started wearing really thick jumpers and coats. By the time the weather had warmed up I had got used to it thank goodness, but the first few times I tried to wear it I would maybe have it on for about an hour then off it came again. God it was uncomfortable, but I got there in the end and when Mum noticed I was wearing it all the time she reluctantly got me another one. Times were hard.

An even worse change was about to come into my life: stockings and suspenders. Putting a bra on was a pushover compared to those. Mum must have figured that this would be the next request I would make. I had lost the vest and now I had to lose the long socks – they just didn't go with a bra, and also I was almost fourteen and everyone at school had them. So Mum took me down the road to the wool shop, which sold wool and lot of other things for ladies, like hankies and bras and stockings and suspenders. I never chose the suspenders, Mum did that, but she did ask me what type of stockings I wanted and of course I wanted the same as every other girl in my school, black diamond pattern. Great, I was getting there.

I went straight up to my bedroom and began working out the best way to put them on, and it was like a puzzle – I just couldn't do it. So I took off most of my clothes and tried again. About an hour later my

Mum came up to see what I was doing for so long and when she saw me stood there almost in knots she howled with laughter and said, "Do you need any help?" The stockings were twisted so tight around my legs I had almost lost all feeling in them, and they had great holes and ladders in them. The suspenders were in completely the wrong place, so I did what I always did – I lost my temper, tore them off and didn't bother with the bloody things again for weeks, but I did get the hang of them eventually, or I would have been the only fourteen-year-old still wearing long socks in my school. But I never liked them, and thank god tights came in some two years later and I cut my suspender belt into pieces. Women's Lib had begun.

When I was almost twelve I started secondary school. It was nowhere near as bad as the middle school had been, and within a few months I had met a girl who was to become my best friend for life, Paula. She was quiet like me and also younger than her years like me; we both began our teenage years so naïve, but we had some fun getting there. We went everywhere together like sisters. When we were thirteen we were really into boys and by the time we were fourteen we were never without a date, although at that time sex was never involved – neither of us was mature enough for that kind of relationship. We just had a good time, like the time we promised to meet two boys outside the pictures and got them to pay for us to go in and when they asked where we would like to sit upstairs or down we said "up", although we never went upstairs, which was where all the old folk went. Anyway, after five minutes of sitting with them we excused ourselves to go to the toilet and went straight downstairs to be with the other teenagers. The boys never came looking for us, so they had a lucky escape. We were always doing things like that, but one time I got caught and the boy that caught me chased me out of the pictures and pushed me into a shop doorway and hit me quite badly. There were people standing at a bus stop looking at what was happening, but no one would help me. Then a car stopped and a guy called out to me to get in, and with that the guy who was hitting me ran off. I knew the guy in the car as he was a member of an older gang that we knew. Anyway he took me home and I went straight to bed. I was very shaken up by what had happened, but I couldn't tell my Dad because he would have made it worse.

I decided I wouldn't do that again, so when I met a boy I liked I stayed with him for a while and didn't two or three time him. I met a boy I had a real crush on and he liked me, so we went out together a few times. Then one day he told me to get lost and I didn't understand why, so the next day I went to his house and he came out and said he would walk me back home. He didn't want to talk to me, and I asked what was wrong. His answer was to get hold of me and shake me and punch me and push me down on the ground, and just for good measure he kicked me. Again I couldn't tell my Dad as I wasn't supposed to have boyfriends and I would get a wallop from him as well. It didn't stop me from having boyfriends, but I had no respect for any of them. I know now that I was looking for someone to love me.

One day I was outside our house with a small group of other kids. We were all about thirteen and I had borrowed my brother's racing bike to be the same as all the others as they all had bikes. My dad was well known by the local kids because he was always shouting at them, and they all steered clear. We were all together behind the garages out of sight, but not up to anything, just talking. I was sitting on my brother's bike and leaning against a boy who was on his bike as well, just to stop myself from falling off.

Then I saw Dad. He came around the back of the garage and everyone ran. He was screaming that he would kill them all. I dropped the bike and ran indoors. I begged this girl who lived over the road from me to come with me. In the dining room I was begging her not to leave me alone with him, as I knew he wouldn't hurt me if she stayed.

He came in in a flaming temper and screamed at

her to get out and she ran, then it started. He chased me into the hall, slapping me all the time. I was terrified and screaming at him "don't hit me, please don't hit me!" I got away and he chased me upstairs. I made the bathroom and locked him out, not that a lock would have stopped him. He pushed the bathroom door in on me and I ran under his arm into my bedroom. I fell onto my bed and he started to hit me so hard and I screamed with pain every time he brought his hand down on me– it seemed to go on forever. Then he just stopped and went downstairs. I hurt all over - there wasn't a single place he had managed to miss.

Like most times when this happened, I have problems recalling what happened next. I remember my mum coming upstairs a lot later on when it was dark and saying "Your dad wants to talk to you", so I went downstairs. He didn't look at me but he looked as though he had been crying, and Mum said, "Your dad says you can have that rabbit you wanted". I said thank you and just went back upstairs and went to bed. I still hurt so much I didn't go out the next day. He got me the rabbit and built a hutch and run for him, and I called him Hoppity and I loved him.

Mum and Dad seemed to hate each other. She was afraid to speak to him, and she threw her whole life into working for her mum and cleaning our house. They didn't argue, but it was the silence in the house that was so awful, everyone afraid to speak or make a noise just in case we upset him. And so life went on. If only she had told someone about it, like her mum or her sister or brother, I know they would have had something to say to him, but he knew she never would. Maybe he had threatened her not to "or else" – that's what he usually did.

One day when I got in from school Mum was waiting for me; she had her coat on and was very upset and seemed frightened. She asked if James was behind me and I didn't know. Then he came through the gate and before he could get inside the door she said, "quick, we have to go". We asked where and she said to Auntie Maggie's. She began to run down the road and so did we and I remember she kept looking over her shoulder and saying, "Hurry up, he is going to kill us." We ran for two miles, half of that uphill. When we got to my auntie's she was out, but the door, like most in those days, was open thank god.

We got in and Mum locked the door behind us. Then, because it was a bungalow, she still didn't feel safe, so she made my brother and me get into the small toilet with her because it had frosted windows and a lock on the door. We had only just made it when we heard a screech of car tyres outside and we knew it was him coming to kill us. I had never seen my mum so afraid. My brother seemed distant, as if he wasn't really there, and I wet myself.

Then he came to the front door and bashed on it. He had to be very drunk, because I know he wouldn't have dared do that on my auntie's door. When he got no answer he came to each of the windows and began banging and shouting, and I was terrified he would break the window and find us and kill us.

After what seemed an eternity, we heard his car pull away. When Mum let us out of the toilet we sat and waited for my auntie to come home. Mum was consumed by what had just happened and I guess she forgot to ask if we were OK, but I knew my brother had had some kind of shutdown. He never spoke; he just came out of the toilet and sat in a chair. Later he said his friends would be waiting for him and asked when we were going.

When my auntie came home, Mum had to let her in because she had locked the door. I don't know what was said, but we were sent out of the room while they talked. I don't remember what happened next, only that my auntie pulled me to one side later and told me that my dad had tried to gas himself and that he had been found and taken to hospital. Apparently when he had left my auntie's he had smashed his car up and gone home and tried to kill himself. All I remember is that when I was told this I thought, good, I hope he dies.

What happened that day was never mentioned again between me and my brother or my mum; that was the way they did things. If you didn't talk about it, it hadn't happened. Maybe they thought we would forget.

The next day was a school day and we got up and went as usual, not speaking about the night before or asking where Dad was, not that we really cared. The thought of being without him was good, and I felt really optimistic about the prospect of life with just my mum and brother. Such peace! We would all be able to relax and my mum would be stop being afraid.

That afternoon when we came home from school, Mum said to us "go upstairs and say goodbye to your dad, he is getting ready to leave".

Great, I thought, let's get this over with, because just the mere thought of looking at him made my stomach lurch. So I went upstairs, not knowing what kind of mood I would find him in; he was in the bathroom having a shave and the door was open. Suddenly I just couldn't speak to him, so as he hadn't noticed me walk past the door I went straight to my room.

After about five minutes I had to do it, I had to be brave, so I came out of my bedroom. He was still in the bathroom, so I went to the door and said very quietly, "bye". He looked over his shoulder at me and said "bye", but he held my eyes and didn't look away, and I felt something I had never felt before for my father, and that was pity. I knew then that he did really love me and he was truly sorry. Oh god, I was so sad and so mixed up. I knew we would all be better off without him, I had been looking forward to it, but now I wasn't sure, I think I knew he needed us.

My mum was very quiet the next day. She never told us where Dad was; she just didn't talk about any of it, so we just thought that was that. Then the following day she told us that Dad was coming home, and that was it, he came home that night. It wasn't a happy occasion – no balloons or banners or party cakes just complete silence as usual. I felt the gloom come over me again and I knew it was because I knew that whatever he did to us he would never leave, and there was no escape from him.

I do believe my respect for both my parents took a dive after this, for my mum because I wondered what he would have to do to make her leave him, and my dad because of how frightened he had made my brother and me that day he chased us, and he had never even said sorry; worse still, he had not even acknowledged it. I hated him again. So life went on from one miserable day to the next. Nothing changed, in fact it seemed to get worse; he was drinking more, I think.

CHAPTER 3

In and out of school

I was getting on OK at school at this point and I had met three girls who I got on with really well, so I had something to look forward to. We used to have a laugh at school. None of us took it seriously and eventually we were moved into the library below stairs, as the teachers had given up on us. It wasn't a real classroom, just somewhere to put us to keep us out of the other more serious girls' way. We did have lessons but to be honest our teacher didn't seem to care much either, we only had about six months left at school, and I remember her sighing quite a lot and telling us to get on with reading our books. There were about eight of us girls who had been banished to the library. I loved it! I had my best mates with me and the four of us all sat at one large round table where we would plan our coming night out, such excitement there was. We had learnt that as long as we said yes or no to the questions thrown at us by the teacher we didn't have to do anything else – after all, she didn't expect us to know anything, so we were not under any pressure.

Two of the girls in the library with us I had previously been bullied by; one was a ringleader and the other one was one of her devoted followers. They picked on me continually for about a year because I was so quiet and had no friends at first. When I had made some friends in my second year my confidence started to grow, not in any big way, but I just wasn't prepared to put up with it any more.

One day as I was going into the science lab for the next lesson I was the first one there, and the classroom was empty. I guess she saw her chance. I didn't see her coming at me until she had her hands clawing at my face with her big long nails. I went a little mad. I practically threw her against a cupboard and she went crashing into it, knocking the doors open so there was ink, rulers, pens, books, chalk, you name it was in there, the lot just fell around her head. I wanted her blood – I had had enough.

Then a prefect came in and stopped it, pulling me

off the bitch. I was so mad I think I must have scared this girl, because although we never became friends, she never bullied me again and she even used to ask me what I was up to after school, but I never wanted to be mates with her; I just wanted her respect, and I got it.

That was a good time for me. I had discovered a new-found inner strength and I felt so grown up. After school I used to dash home, get my tea and quickly get ready to rush back to my best friend's house, and then we would both go on to our next friend's house. I lived farthest away from the town so I started off first. It was all uphill, almost vertical, but it didn't bother me, I was young, and I practically ran up it in my excitement to get out.

Right at the top and opposite our school was Paula's house; she was and still is my best friend. I used to call for her every morning for school. I would always be welcomed by her mum, who was a lovely lady and so friendly, completely different from my mum. I loved going in to see her. She would always say how pretty I was and how I reminded her of Elizabeth Taylor. Let me tell you, I was not used to any sort of compliment, let alone such a fantastic one as that!

I loved her so much, and It was a love that was to deepen over the years to come. I would cry in frustration sometimes because she wasn't my mum and I wanted her to be. I wasn't jealous of Paula, but I would get a little envious sometimes, the way her mum used to want to know where we were going that night, who we had met, if the boys had been good looking or 'ugly beasts', as she would call them. She was always interested in what we wore and our make-up (lots of Pan-Stick and black eyeliner). She loved it. You would think she was coming out with us sometimes, but it was just the pure pleasure she got from us having a good time which was so lovely and at the same time so alien to me.

I on the other hand used to get ready in my bedroom and just leave the house. No one ever asked where I was going or what I was wearing - I don't think they even looked. I think they just assumed that I went out with my friends most evenings. I did have a curfew though and that was ten-thirty and I must say I was always back on time, probably because of the thought of my dad coming looking for me.

So I would get to Paula's and bask in the compliments, and it became like my second home. Paula's house was the halfway house, you could call it, to town, and once we were sure we couldn't look any better without being able to smile for fear of cracking the Pan-Stick, we left for Janet's – she actually lived in town. She was always ready to run out of the door and off we would go. We walked everywhere. We either headed for the bowling alley, though we never played a game because it was just a meeting place for some kids, or if it was a weekend we could go to the local flea pit or the Palace as it was called. And for two and six, which was my weekly pocket money, I could get in and buy ten Embassy and share them with Janet. Paula hated smoking and never did try it.

We always went downstairs and it was a riot. Nobody ever watched the film unless it had a bit of sex in it, which wasn't likely then. Paula and I used to like the Rockers in those days and we used to try to be like them. They were always in the Palace on Sundays, pulling the arms off of the seats so that they could get closer to their girlfriends. We used to hear a loud CRACK and everyone would cheer and shout because they knew what was happening. The poor old usherette used to run, or hobble, depending on which one had been brave enough to take the Sunday night shift, to where she thought the noise had come from, shining her torch on lots of innocent-looking faces – they never got caught. I did wonder if they didn't care because in the next few years they were going to pull the place down. Maybe they thought if they let us pull enough bits off it would save them money.

My hair at the time was extremely backcombed – the bigger the hair the better, that was the fashion. I backcombed for about an hour and then smoothed the top over very carefully. I used a knitting needle to pull it up and out, then finally half a can of hairspray to glue it all in place. It was as stiff as a board and nothing could move it, not even a gale. With my white face, black eyes and black ratted hair I looked amazing. All I needed was a leather jacket with studs on it, but I wasn't allowed one, so Paula and I started to nick the studs off the Rockers' leathers while they were hanging on pegs just inside the door of the Red Cow pub next to the Palace. We used to pop our heads just inside the door because we were still too young to go into pubs and watch these gorgeous guys drink beer and play bar billiards. They soon got to know us and thought we were sweet, so we were invited into the pub. God, my dad would have killed me and them. But the guys were really nice and they never took advantage of us. We must have looked like such young kids, but we were feeling so grown up. Before we left to go home we would take a few souvenirs off their jackets, a chain one week, a stud the next, a tiger tail the next – if they knew it was us, they never said.

After about six months of this pilfering we could have opened a small market stall with it, but we were keeping it all for the leather jackets that we would be getting soon. We never got the jackets. Life has a way of twisting and turning, and it doesn't matter how much you kick against it you are carried along with the flow.

One night sticks in my mind and in Paula's too, as we were laughing about it the just other day. We were asked by two boys we had known for some time if we would like to go to a party, and not only that, they would take us on their bikes. Well of course we said yes. We didn't have the appropriate gear for riding pillion and we didn't realize that the really tight skirts we were wearing just wouldn't allow you to straddle a motor bike seat. My skirt was quite a bit tighter than Paula's, but I wasn't going to let a little thing like a skirt get in my way. So the boy got on the bike and while his back was turned I hitched my skirt up to the top of my suspenders and got on. We were off racing through the town, no crash helmets, not that one would have fitted on top of my hair. The wind was trying its best to rush through my hair, but not really succeeding.

Out of town we went, and up a really steep hill. I knew the party was up there somewhere, but what I wasn't expecting was that the rider took a short cut through a hedge and across a field, and screeched to a halt outside the house. My hair was ruined. There were bits of hedge in it, along with thorns and leaves, my face was scratched and a bit of blood was merging with my Pan-Stick. My beautiful black eye makeup was all over my cheeks, my stockings were shredded, and to top it all the really tight skirt that I had run in by hand to get it as tight as possible was about burst. You could see the white cotton stitches straining (it was the only colour I could find at the time, the skirt was red) and any further sudden movement would have meant it coming off completely, something I couldn't have dealt with, not with my oh so cool image (still there, just about).

I pretended that everything was just fine and we went into the party. I had to ask for the toilet, which was really embarrassing because girls didn't need to use to toilets in those days, just as we didn't fart either. Paula didn't rat her hair up, so she came off with much less damage than me. But you know I came out of that toilet like a phoenix rising from the ashes, and on motorbikes I was hooked. My hair did take a bit of a beating though, not only with my brush, but it seemed to hold a certain fascination for some people. When we were at the Palace some weekends nobody would sit behind me. I used to hear them say in a whisper "I'll have to move, I can't see over her hair". Then there were some nights I used to get home after a film only to have to sit for ages picking out the peanuts in my beehive because they had used it for target practice. Thank goodness it was a hairstyle that didn't last long.

After that all that was to be found in my hair was daisies, because flower power had arrived. I have some really good memories from that time. One of them was on a Saturday night when I used to get home around ten thirty and my Dad would have cooked a macaroni cheese, especially for me and him. I can still see him getting it out of the oven all bubbly and hot and dripping melted cheese down the side of the dish – the smell was delicious. I was always on time for this as he always did things on time. My Dad had never cooked a thing in his life but he found this recipe on the back of a tin of tomato soup and it became a regular Saturday night treat. I don't remember my brother eating it – maybe he didn't like it –and needless to say my mum wouldn't have touched it because she hadn't cooked it, so it might poison her. So it was just for me and Dad, and it's one of my best memories. He stopped cooking it after we moved away a couple of years later, and he never cooked anything ever again.

Hoppity was doing OK, but as I got older I paid less attention to him. I think my mum had taken over the role of feeding him, I can't remember. I do know that in those days animals were treated more like animals, so he wasn't brought in when it was freezing cold, although he did have his hutch to keep him warm. Whether he had enough straw was another matter. Mum wasn't a real animal lover and Dad was always at work, so I guess he was a bit neglected.

Anyway, one day I went down to the bottom of the garden to see him, I remember it was a really hot day, and I noticed a large lump on his face, and when I felt it he squirmed in my hands, so he must have been in a lot of pain. I went to tell Mum and Dad, and Dad said it must be an abscess, so I thought he would have to go to the vet and as you do when you are young you believe that your parents will sort it all out and it will be OK, so nothing more was said.

The next day Mum, James and I were going to South-end with my Nan and her boyfriend, who had one of those little chocolate box cars from way back in the twenties or thirties. We were kind of excited but getting to an age where you didn't really want to show it. I thought I would just go and check on Hoppity, and when I looked in the run he was stretched out and cold and stiff – he must have died in agony. I was so terribly upset. Mum didn't handle feelings, so I had to go along to the seaside as planned and pretend to be happy. I guess it wasn't their fault he had died, but I blamed them anyway. I was old enough to understand that they hadn't really bothered with him, and he should have gone to the vet's. That was the last rabbit I ever had myself. They had been such a big part of my life, but I must have been starting to grow up.

Another very sad memory for me was when my cat Sandy, who I had had for about twelve years, suddenly developed an abscess on his throat and it burst and left a big tear in his skin. He was trying to drink some milk and it was coming through this gaping wound in his neck – I was horrified. When I went indoors to tell Mum what had happened, she was in one chair and my dad was in the opposite chair either side of the fireplace, which was something they never did together, in fact they did nothing together. I sat down at the dining table and my mum said Sandy had an abscess and needed to go to the vet to be put to sleep, as there was nothing they could do for him.

I put my head in my hands and cried uncontrollably, but after a couple of minutes I realized that I was on my own, as they had both got up and left the room. I didn't even get a comforting hand on my shoulder, nothing, they just left me to my grief alone. Whether they took him to the vet's or whether my Dad just put him out of his misery himself I will never know, but I like to think he just drifted off to sleep peacefully and humanely. My dear lovely Sandy, I still think of you and Hoppity.

CHAPTER 4

End of innocence

~elle~

So life went on. Around my fourteenth birthday my brother, who was twelve was getting into all sorts of trouble at school. He was playing truant continuously and mixing with all the wrong types. My mum managed to keep this a secret from Dad because she knew how he would handle it, with a bloody good hiding, and her nerves were just not up to it. But one afternoon my dad came home from work early and there was a phone call from the school asking where James was. My dad asked questions and was told that he hadn't been in school for three weeks. Well that was it; my dad was out for my brother's blood, and probably my mum's as well for not telling him. It was just one of those things.

I had never played truant before that day, but Paula and I decided to skip our last lesson of the day, so we ran out of school and got to the top of the hill and had started down it to run to my house when we heard Matron's voice screaming, "Girls, come back right now!" We looked round and there she was in her stiff white apron and white hat holding on to it for dear life in case it blew off, and her skirt billowing out around her showing her black stocking tops. She actually didn't look much of a threat and she was really quite a nice woman, but the Headmistress, now that was a different story, we all lived in dread of her and her cane. So with heads lowered we walked back up the hill and were escorted back into school and taken straight to the Headmistress.

Matron went in first and after about two minutes she came out and sent us in. God, my heart was nearly jumping out of my chest, as I knew what was coming. She asked who was the oldest of us and I squeaked "Me, Miss, "so with that she dispatched Paula back to class with a warning, but kept me there. I thought I was going to faint as I watched her go to the big tall cupboard in the corner where everyone knew she kept The Cane. She took it from the cupboard and walked back over to me, swishing it as she came, and told me to hold my hand out. When I did so she said, "No not flat like that, hold it like this" and she took my hand and turned it sideways so she could aim for the knuckle of my thumb, and she got it five times. God, it hurt like hell! It immediately swelled up. It was on a scar where a year earlier I had had stitches. While rolling out some pastry for one of my famous lemon meringue pies with an empty milk bottle (we didn't possess a rolling pin) I had lost my temper because the pastry kept sticking to the bottle, so I smacked it down on top of the Rolls twin tub washing machine which I was using as a table top and it cut into my thumb quite deeply – I had forgotten I was holding a glass.

After school I said to Paula how unfair it was that she had got away with it just because she was eight months younger than me, and we decided that we wouldn't try it again as we were really no good at it and it wasn't worth the hassle.

Anyway, all this happened the same day as my dad found out about my brother's truancy. I found out later that that same afternoon he had taken another phone call from my school to say I had left school without permission. He must have gone a bit crazy in the head while he waited for us to get home from school, and guess who got home first? I didn't see him coming, there were no questions, no whys, just another attack. He hit, he slapped, and he grabbed my arm so I couldn't get away. He hit me again and again until I managed to break free and flee in fear of my life. The only way I could go was upstairs. There was no time to open a door and run – he ran after me and it began again, hitting and slapping so hard you could see the welts coming up. I think he wanted to kill me, and the only way he could stop himself was to keep hitting me until his anger died down a bit. Then he stopped beating me and just walked off downstairs. It seemed like he had been hitting me for half an hour, but it must have been more like five minutes. I was completely exhausted, having been trying to fight him off and protect my head and face at the same time, and I still didn't know why.

Then in came Mum. I heard him shout at her, but I was in too much shock to take much notice. Everything went quiet again then in came my brother. I never heard him get shouted at or hit. I thought that someone might come up and see me, but they didn't.

I got off my bed, stiff and sore, and started to get ready to go out as I had planned to. I got changed out of my uniform, put on my going-out-to-find-a-boy clothes and set off for Paula's. I left the house without anybody trying to stop me or ask how I was. I never mentioned it to Paula as it was something I didn't want to relive in my mind, so I just shoved it somewhere in the back of my head and left it there, something I became good at doing.

When I got home, around the usual time, Mum and Dad were sitting watching the TV. I didn't go into the sitting room I just went straight to bed and slept. Next day Dad had gone to work and Mum was getting ready to go to work herself. There was still no concern about how I was, and do you know something – I began to think that my dad's behaviour was normal and it was just me making a fuss.

Anyway when I got home that afternoon my Mum mentioned the phone calls from the school he had had, and said that from now on she wouldn't be able to stop him from checking up, so we had to behave ourselves or else. She also said "Your dad said that that good hiding had been meant for James, and I had got what he should have had because I was home first". Oh, that was all right then! I wondered if he would offer to buy me another rabbit, but he didn't. "Sorry" would have been nice though.

Things seemed to get worse at home, if that was possible. No laughing, no talking out loud, no playing or having fun of any kind allowed. It was so bad that you couldn't even look at him without fear of his hand being raised or putting his hands to his belt in preparation of taking it off, life was so miserable. We went out as much as we could to get away from the oppressive atmosphere.

It's taken me over fifty years to admit that my young life wasn't normal. It's a relief to write about it and get it all out of me, but there is also an enormous amount of guilt in doing so, because as I said I did love my mum and dad and I feel that now they're gone they can't defend themselves, but It's something I've had to do for my own peace. I know things were bad between my parents because of the silence between them, but there were never any arguments, as she knew better. I guess Mum did as we did – she kept her head down and didn't speak. That might sound like a huge exaggeration to those of my family that knew him, or thought they did, but it's true.

Needless to say, without proper guidance and no one to talk to at home we were getting into all sorts of scrapes. My brother was expelled from his all-boys' school because of continued truancy and the strange thing was my dad never lost his temper with him; I don't know whether he had given up on us or if he didn't want to beat one of his children again. As I said, I think he really wanted to kill me that day and I don't think he could trust his self, I think it was the latter.

Anyway, James was sent to a mixed school and did get on better, but he still had time off. When he was fifteen he left school and had a couple of jobs which he never stayed at, and then one day he packed a backpack and left home to go travelling around

Scotland with one of his friends. He was gone a few weeks, but he came home for money, food etc. And then he was gone again, guitar on his back, mouth organ in his pocket. He loved music and had taught himself to play and read and write it from the age of twelve. He was a very talented musician. Even to this day I still meet some of his friends from way back in the sixties, most of them in bands themselves, and they always say he had led the way for them. I know how proud that makes me feel and how sorry for him I am that Dad never gave him any praise. He didn't recognize that his son had such talent, he hated his music and didn't allow him to play indoors, so when he was at home he used to go into the shed at the top of the garden and play. Sometimes when he played his bass guitar and the speakers were turned right up, you could see the roof and walls of the little wooden shed shake. That was OK, Dad was already going deaf at that time so it didn't bother him, plus it was usually when he was on night work. James mainly played the acoustic guitar he had learned on, mouthorgan around his neck on a piece of wire and his Jew's harp of course, singing *Blowing In The Wind* and lots of other Bob Dylan songs. Dylan was his favourite for a long time, but as he grew up he played more of Jimi Hendrix and lots of heavy rock – I didn't really care for it, I used to like Bob better. He grew his hair, which was blond and straight – how I envied him that hair, mine being black and wavy – and he wore a fur waistcoat with nothing underneath except a tie, bell bottom jeans with a huge belt around them and what they used to call 'bumpers' on his feet that looked as if they were about to fall off at any moment, they were so tatty. We did kind of drift apart, with him never being at home and me out at every opportunity, but we were to come back together again when I left home.

One evening in March while I was walking home with Paula, a white van pulled up alongside us, two boys in the front and one in the back. They offered us a lift home and they were so good looking we just couldn't help ourselves, so we climbed into the back of the van.

And so, at the ripe old age of fifteen, began the end of my childhood. The boy driving seemed to really fancy me, but I can't say the same for him. The boy in the passenger seat was OK, but the boy in the back was gorgeous and he liked me too, so we began to go out together. His name was Dick and I developed the most enormous crush on him. He was four years older than me, had been to the local grammar school and was very clever. He could drive and he had a job in a lab. He also wore a suit all the time and looked so grown up. I was still at school, and Dick quite often used to be waiting for me outside the gates at home time. I felt so grown up – my boyfriend had a car and was waiting for me and all my school mates could see me get into this car with this really gorgeous boy. My mum knew that I was seeing him but she thought he was too old for me, so she didn't tell my dad for a while, in fact it was April, when I left school, before she told him, a month later. In March I was too young to have a boyfriend but in April I was old enough! No wonder I used to get confused.

Anyway he was all right about it because I had left school and was now deemed completely grown up. I had a job lined up in the Co-op hairdressers in town – I had always liked to play around with hair and had even cut friends' hair and styled it, and they were always pleased with what I did for them, so it seemed only natural to become a hairdresser. That was until one of my friends asked me how much money I was going to get each week and I said two pounds and ten shillings and she just gawped at me and said "I'll be getting six pounds ten a week!" So I went with her to work in a factory –and hated every minute of it. I had to be up at five am to walk a mile to the bus stop to get into town for six thirty to catch the coach that would take us another fifteen miles to work in a perfume factory and clock on at 7 am, and then do the whole thing again at 5.30 to get home. I stuck it for two weeks.

I don't remember telling my mum that I had left the job, just that I had started a new one, this time in an electrical factory. I quite liked this job as the girls were very friendly and I knew one from school, and she and I paled up together. One afternoon in the summer we decided to go to the local park after our lunch break and not go back to work – we got away with it by saying I had been really unwell after lunch and she had had to take me home. Then about a week later I decided to try it again on my own, but this time I was seen by someone from work, and when I got in the next day I was called into the office and given the sack.

That really was a shock. I didn't think it could happen – I thought that if I did get caught I would just get told off. I had managed to last at that job for six weeks. I had to tell my mum what had happened, and she was disappointed, I could tell, but she didn't tell Dad. Anyway my uncle told my mum that there were jobs going in his factory if I was interested, so off I went for an interview. I did get the job but I felt sick most days in there – the smell of the glue and stuff they used was awful, although nobody else seemed bothered by it. I was really unhappy there. Nobody spoke to me. It was a huge place and I used to wander around in my breaks on my own outside, trying to get the smell of glue fumes out of my nose. I felt so unwell and nauseous. I dreaded going in each day and after about a month I told my Mum that I couldn't work there any more as the smell was making me feel sick. She said I would have to look for another job straight away, but I still didn't feel well.

What I didn't know was that I was pregnant – it wasn't just the smell in the factory. Fifteen and three months pregnant, but I still didn't know what was wrong with me. I began to feel better a few weeks down the road, and Mum just assumed it had been something I had picked up, but then she was on my case again about looking for another job. Dick and I were still going strong. I thought I loved him and I think he thought he loved me. So one evening he took me up to London and to a friend of his who dealt in second-hand jewellery and bought me a ring. It was a diamond solitaire and I hung it around my neck until I could pluck up the courage to tell my parents that we were engaged. I thought I would tell them when I was sixteen, which was just a few months away. It was now October 1966. My mum, looking rather worried, pulled me to one side and asked me if I was still having my periods, and I said no. I still didn't have a clue. She asked me how long it had been since my last one and I said quite a while, so she took me to the doctor's. The doctor, whom I had known all my life, examined me and said to my mum, "Susanne is about five months pregnant".

I thought my mum was going to pass out. The doctor became concerned about her and got her a drink of water. He told her to get me an appointment at the hospital as soon as possible as I was so far gone. You would have thought I wasn't there. None of it made sense to me, although the movements I had kept feeling in my stomach were beginning to make sense.

When we left to go home she didn't speak to me at first, then, after a while she told me what was happening to me. She used a totally different voice, like the one she used when talking to an adult. I didn't recognize her and that scared me, because if ever I needed my mum it was now. But she changed towards me overnight. She was quite distant from me and adopted a 'You've made your bed...' kind of attitude. My dad still didn't know till some weeks later.

Dick was as naïve as me. When I told him, he didn't react much; it was as though it wasn't real to either of us. We were both as immature as each other, just kids. In those days some things weren't spoken about, especially sex. I don't know how our parents expected us to avoid situations like getting pregnant when it was a taboo subject, and his parents were as anally retentive as mine.

We started by fumbling around, the blind leading the blind but we eventually got the hang of it, after which there was no stopping us. This might sound hard to believe, but he really was as ignorant as me. We knew the basics of course, but not quite how you could get pregnant, a recipe for disaster. When I think about how much the kids of today know it's shameful to think we were that naïve. Although I hadn't had my periods for some months I wasn't worried, I just didn't think about it. I didn't connect it with pregnancy, and what was pregnancy anyway? It really was that bad.

Around this time my dad was painting my old wooden wardrobe and dressing table for me. I don't remember asking him to do this so my mum must have said it needed brightening up in my bedroom now I was fifteen. He was very good at painting, and the colour Mum had chosen was lilac and white. It looked lovely when he had finished it, and I was so pleased. They seemed to be taking an interest in my room and treating me as more grown up. I couldn't wait to show it off to my friends. My pregnancy didn't seem real– I was never going to have a baby. How could I? It was all a mistake.

Dad had painted my bedroom furniture in the shed and when it was finished he got me to help him lift it back upstairs into my room. I remember my mum saying to him "Jim, I can do that, Susanne you stand there." Was she mad? Of course I could help; I didn't realize that because I was almost six months pregnant she was afraid I would hurt myself. Anyway it was after this that she told me that Dick had to tell my Dad as soon as he could. She said it would be a good idea to tell him next Tuesday evening.

Tuesday evening came and we sat in Dick's left-hand-drive bright yellow Renault for about an hour outside the local pub trying to pluck up courage to go and tell him. I felt ill with worry. This was really happening. At last the enormity of the situation was beginning to dawn on me. There actually was a baby growing inside me. I couldn't go, I was too afraid, he had to go on his own, and so off he went. Mum had been waiting for us for over two hours and must have been dreading the moment we came in the door.

I had waited in the car for about half an hour when Dick came back. He got in the car and seemed perfectly OK. He said that by the time he had got to my house my mum had already told my dad, and that it looked as if he had been crying. He had told Dick to go and fetch me home. When I got into the front room where they were both sitting down, I thought I should just turn and run and should never have gone back home. My dad looked at me and said that we would have to get married and then he went to get up and attack Dick, but Mum found the courage to push him back. My dad said, "Just because I haven't got up and beat the hell out of you, because believe me I want to, doesn't mean I like you or I'll ever forgive you for what you've done".

That was that, it was over. I was taken to the hospital for a checkup and Mum planned a wedding for December 10th, two days after my sixteenth birthday. Up till then I hadn't really shown that I was pregnant, then all of a sudden I had a bump – quite a neat little bump, but big enough to stop me from wearing my normal clothes.

Mum knew a lady, a friend of the family, who was a seamstress, and she took me over to her to get me measured for a couple of maternity dresses. I still remember the care and concern in June's eyes for me, and shock and pity as well; I had known her all my life and had gone to school with her son. I was probably the only fifteen-year-old she had ever made a maternity dress for and I was her friend's daughter. It was still a time when things like that were hidden away.

I remember one day a neighbour who lived across the road from us knocked on our back door. My Mum said "Quick its old Mrs. Smithfield, don't let her see you," and she pushed me into the corner of the kitchen. Well our back door was half frosted glass and the kitchen was tiny, and as Mum opened the door to Mrs. Smithfield she was looking through the glass and I knew she could see me or the outline of someone. She asked Mum if she could borrow some sugar, so Mum quickly put some in a cup for her, trying not to let the door come open any further. When the woman tried to come in, I thought, bloody cheek that was the first time she had ever been to our house in the seven years we had been there. There was my mum trying to push her back out – I had never seen such cheek. I heard her ask Mum how I was and Mum said "Susanne is fine, she's out at the moment and I'm I the middle of doing my washing if you don't mind I'm busy." With that the nosey old cow went away. When my Mum closed the door she said "That's it, she must have seen you outside at sometime, she knows". I was now being smuggled in and out of the house, usually after dark.

By the end of November we had moved house, miles away to the country, where we knew no one, and more importantly no one knew us. Mum bought me some yellow wool and a knitting pattern for a baby's layette set, which was what we all had for our babies in those days. It consisted of a matinee jacket, a bonnet, booties and mittens. Mum had taught me to knit some years ago when I was about six, although she almost gave up on it because I used both my right and left hand to write and I did the same with knitting, so consequently I would knit the stitches onto one needle and then knit them off again, if that makes sense, so I always had one row and no more. This went on for almost two years and I can still hear her saying in frustration, "It's pointless, she will never get the hang of it," but eventually I got it and became good at it. All day I would sit knitting until it was done. Then I got my favourite doll, Christine her name was, a baby doll, and dress her up in the baby clothes. I left them on her and put her in the sideboard, getting her out now and then and thinking how lovely she looked. I don't know if Mum knew I did this. If I had been her I would have worried about my daughter. I had never had any contact with babies and knew nothing about them I just had to learn as I went along.

The wedding day was approaching fast and Mum bought me a blue maternity dress, which was very nice, but it itched liked mad because it was made of some god-awful material that only ever existed in the sixties I expect, a rough kind of wool mixture, with what felt like bits of wire wool woven into it that prickled and itched at the same time. I can't remember what Dick wore – probably his brown suit. The ceremony was quick, thank god. I was so embarrassed about it all that I couldn't say the word 'solemnly', I just couldn't, and in a fit of nerves I turned round and laughed out loud to my Mum, who just glared at me for showing her up and acting like a child.

Then it was back to his parents' house for a buffet, no wedding cake for me, no music, no laughter. Only two pictures were taken, but my dad got rid of them years later. It was freezing cold out and raining like mad and inside was just as glum. No honeymoon for me, no beautiful bride's dress or bridesmaids, no gifts, no cards except one from my Auntie Maggie and Uncle Mick and I still have it, it was to wish me luck, and boy was I going to need it.

We moved in with my parents and we were given the smallest bedroom, two single beds one on each side of the room and a carry cot placed exactly in the middle of them, ready for the new arrival. I spent my days knitting and dressing my dolls and Dick sometimes went to work. He was in fact bone idle; my dad called him lethargic, among other things and as you can imagine it didn't exactly make for happy families. You could have cut the air with a knife, it was awful. Most of the time he lied and said that he had been to work, but on several occasions he was seen by a friend or family member out and about with his mates. I discovered a few years later that he was a perpetual liar and he even believed himself, so convincing was he, and of course when you're that good a liar everyone else believes you. Up till then I had had no experience with liars, so I was sucked in like everyone else. He must care, he must be working, he really loves me... I got so I hated my mum and dad for keeping on at him. He was trying his best after all, wasn't he?

I was having regular checkups at the hospital, and just before the last one my feet and hands swelled up so much I couldn't get my shoes on, or my rings. I felt giddy and had a headache and I told my mum, who always came with me, that I didn't think I would bother going, but she insisted and gave me a pair of Dad's slippers to put on my swollen feet. Feeling mortified didn't even come close to how I felt about this. I had to tramp across a field to the bus stop and stand there for fifteen minutes in the freezing January weather waiting for the bus (which was always either late or early, so you always tried to get there at an in-between time), feeling hideous in these great big old floppy tartan, (yep, that's right, tartan) men's slippers and thinking everyone was looking at me. Oh dear God, please just kill me now, I kept thinking. But He didn't. When the bus came I sat downstairs quickly tucking my feet under the seat in front of me – at least I could relax for fifteen minutes or so. It always got worse for me; we got off the bus in the HIGH STREET! And it was a Friday and all the market stalls were out and loads of people.

I plodded alongside my mum with my eyes focusing on the pavement for at least another fifteen minutes, praying not to see anyone I knew. To get to the hospital the last part of the journey was up a very steep hill, and by then I felt so unwell I was past caring, I just needed to lie down. When we got inside we joined all the other expectant mums all sitting in a row knitting and smoking and chatting, waiting to be seen. It always seemed to go quiet when I walked in with my mum. There was no appointment system in those days, which was why they all sat in a line, first come first seen.

I must have been waiting for twenty minutes when the midwife called me in. She weighed me and then took my blood pressure, looked at me and then took it again, and called for a doctor. He came and took my blood pressure and then told me to get on the couch and relax. He asked me if I had come with anyone and I said my mum, so he got the midwife to go and call her in. The doctor explained to me and Mum that my blood pressure was extremely high and they were going to admit me at once. He said "She needs a good rest". My mum looked amazed at him and said "A good rest, she doesn't do anything all day!" It was poor old Mum that did everything indoors, and worked a full day as well. She only had to ask me and I would help, but she was always the same, she preferred to do things her way and if I had offered to help she would have just gone behind me and done it again.

So without further ado I was whisked away in an ambulance to the maternity home, leaving my mum to go home and come back later with my nightdress and other bits. In those days you didn't need to take much in, if anything, for the baby, it was all supplied for you.

I think I took a safety pin for the nappies and that was all.

As soon as I got there I was given a gown to put on and made to get straight into bed, where they took my blood pressure again, after which the midwife went away and came back with some tablets. I was in a ward where women had either had their babies or were still waiting; they used to talk about bumps or babies. I don't remember much for the next few days apart from being woke up for more tablets. I didn't know at the time they were sleeping tablets to keep me still to try and bring down my blood pressure.

After about a week the swelling still hadn't gone down, so they told me they were going to induce me, as I had preeclampsia and the baby had to be delivered as soon as possible. So that afternoon I was taken to a labour ward, not having a clue what was going to happen. There were four midwives with me and one said, with no emotion whatsoever, "We are going to break your waters", and with that she grabbed hold of one leg while the other grabbed the other. They pulled them apart and more or less sat on them, while one of them lay right across my chest and arms. The last one had a glove on and I swear it felt like she had just inserted her whole hand and part of her arm as well into me. I screamed and tried to move, but the midwives must have been used to this because they me held down so fast that all I could move was my head and mouth, it wasn't quick either. Then, without an "Are you all right?" or anything, I was taken back to the ward as if none of it had ever happened.

I do just want to say, for the benefit of any young girls who might read this, that when this happened to me it was 1967. I have since had three more children and I can assure you it is quite different today, with all the pain relief, and the care is so much better.

I had a visitor that evening – Dick's mum. Oh, I think I forgot to mention that during my three weeks' stay in the maternity home Dick never came to see me once. Anyway I was getting excited about having the baby, and when they told me that it would be born soon, I took this literally. I told his mum this with all the knowledge and wisdom of an old pro at having babies and I remember her saying to me "I shouldn't get your hopes up too much Susanne it may not be born until sometime tomorrow."

"What? No, you must be wrong" I said. "They have already done this thing to me and they said it will be born soon." She just smiled at me and didn't talk about it. After that we chatted and I wanted to ask her where her son was, but she was such a nice, gentle lady I didn't want to upset her.

By 8 pm all the visitors had gone home and I was wondering where this baby was – it should have arrived by now. I didn't know about labour and the pain I was going to get, as nobody had told me. I think I must have thought that they just slid out.

I had no pain until about ten that evening, and then it was just the odd twinge now and then. Right, I thought, this is it. By 12.30 am the pain was a lot worse, so they took me down to the delivery room and left me in there on my own, and said try and get some sleep. Try and get some sleep? The woman had to be mad! She had also said that the baby wouldn't be born until the morning and it was only 12.30 am. What was happening?

I started crying uncontrollably and kept ringing the bell for someone to come into me. When a nurse came she said the same thing, try and get some sleep. I knew then that they were all completely mad.

Then the pain got worse, and I was so frightened, I didn't know pain like that existed. I kept crying and calling for my mum, and they kept coming in and trying to calm me down. Then after about an hour a doctor came in. He didn't say anything to me, just gave an injection in my arm I think and left. I don't remember anything else until I was woken up by a midwife telling me that my baby was about to be born and I needed to slide over onto the delivery table. I was surrounded by four or maybe five midwives and a doctor.

I don't remember much about the birth. I guess the injection they gave me was still helping. All I remember was them telling me to push as hard as I could, then feeling as though I was going to split in two and after some pulling and tugging and screaming from me, she was born, my little girl, Jane. She was perfect all 6lbs 4oz of her. She was twenty-one and a half inches long with a mop of black hair and she only gave one quiet little cry.

They counted her fingers and toes in front of me. Her feet and hands were blue and she had to be taken and put into an incubator, so I didn't get to hold her. After they had sorted me out they took me back to the ward and gave me some more sleeping tablets. All I remember about the next few days was being woken up to see Jane – they had wheeled her in in the incubator. They would open the flap at the side and tell me I could touch her little hand then take her away again. After maybe three days she was out of danger and in the nursery with all the other babies, and at feed time, which was every four hours on the dot, the midwives, each carrying two babies, would pass them to their mums to be fed. Most at that time were breast fed, and if not a bottle of Cow & Gate formula was brought in for you to give your baby. I remember the old glass feeding bottles with the old rubber teats on them that had been boiled to death over the years, just like the terry nappies, and the long nightdresses and vests that all the babies were supplied with, all boiled up and dried and put away in an enormous cupboard along with the sheets and towels for baby, all boiled up and as stiff as cardboard.

Feeding time for me was difficult. I was still being given tablets and so they woke me up every few hours to feed her. I don't remember saying I wanted to breast feed, but that was what I was doing, and god it hurt. I complained, but they told me to stick with it. I thought I was getting it all wrong as everyone else seemed to be managing well enough. I wasn't shown how to do it; I just watched the other mothers, but it still didn't feel right. Some of those midwives were pure evil. They didn't like me, I had been a bad girl and I didn't deserve to be liked (some didn't have children themselves and had never experienced childbirth or breast feeding). I would now love to remind them just how they treated this poor young girl in 1967, making her feel more of a freak than ever.

I do remember, though I was in a kind of foggy haze, when a new woman was put in the bed next to me, and the midwife saying to her while pointing at me "This is Susanne, she wakes up now and then, we have her sedated so she won't remember you". I smiled weakly and said hello. That woman turned out to be my life saver when I eventually came round. She was very friendly and we talked for hours as we were confined to bed for the first few days after delivery. She already had three children and had just had the fourth; she had grey hair and lots of lines on her face, so although she was only twenty-six, she looked about sixty to me. Oh god, I thought, this is what having all those kids will do to you in the end, and It really did scare me. Now, looking back, she was ten years younger than my mum –she was only old in my very young eyes.

After five days we were allowed to get up and were moved to another part of the hospital where all the mothers were on their final days of confinement. Most of the day it was going into the lounge area to smoke and drink tea or coffee. There was always a cloud of thick dense smoke in there, and you almost had to feel for a chair to sit in. In between the coughing and chatting I found I was alone again and felt as if I stuck out like a sore thumb, so I used to duck in there quickly and have a tea, I guess hoping someone would talk to me, and duck out again and go back to my bed and my knitting. I was knitting a bottle green cardigan for Dick, but the arm was getting strangely long, I had the buttons ready to go on the needle ready to sew it up, but so far all I had done was a sleeve and it was just getting longer by the hour – I just wasn't concentrating.

I was so unhappy. Why didn't someone come and see me? Every time I looked at a midwife she was looking at me and talking to a mum about me. I heard one of the mothers say to a midwife one day while staring straight at me, "so young", as if I wasn't there. I was sick of it. I just wanted so much to get out of there.

Then when I thought things couldn't get any worse, an auxiliary who used to come in every morning with bowls of water for us to wash with placed my bowl on my bed, and asked me for my flannel. I gave it to her and she put it in the water, took it out dripping wet, stood back and threw It at me. It hit me in the face. Even here I was getting bullied. I just cried, and she laughed and told me to grow up as it was just a joke. All the women on the ward had seen her do this. I wanted to die of shame because of my inability to stand up for myself, and I knew she had targeted me because she knew she would get away with it.

So began my loathing of midwives and my fear of all adults, and my understanding that this was what it was all about for me. I began to expect nothing different from life. If someone did me a wrong I would apologize to them. I sometimes do it now, although not very often, it's just a knee jerk reaction from all those years ago, saying sorry for existing. Example: if someone by pure accident bumps into me I say sorry, it's out if my mouth before I can think about it, a natural response for me, I am saying sorry for being in their way.

One day in a supermarket a few years ago, I was stood looking at some dresses hanging on the rack when I had an awful pain in the back of my foot. I screeched in pain and turned around to see a large, ugly, greasy-haired woman had pushed her shopping trolley into me. She just stared at me as if to say" get out of my way". I almost started to say sorry, but she opened her mouth and asked me why I hadn't seen her trying to get past me. OK, so it was my fault again. She could have just asked me to please move, but she thought she had the god-given right to just try and ram me out of the way.

I know now that the old saying 'the red mist came down' is true – it happened to me that day back in June 1996 in Tesco. I spun round on my heels and got as close to her face as I could and screamed "Do you think I have eyes in the back of my fucking head, you nasty fucking fat ugly bitch?" and lots more of the same. I remember the look on her face as she tried to stand up to me, but I could see I had scared her. I think she thought I was raving mad, which I was at the time –I did want to kill the woman. After that day I realized that I had the power to defend myself, even if it was the wrong way to go about it. It worked and it was the only way I knew, just like dear old Dad.

My last week in the maternity home was so miserable; in three weeks I think I had four visits between Mum and my mother in law, and still no sign of Dick. I was still having difficulty with breast feeding and getting no help with it.

One day we were taken into the nursery and taught how to bath baby, and one by one after we had watched the midwife test the water with her elbow (I found that really strange) and bath a doll, we bathed our babies. The midwife actually praised me and said I had done really well – that was the only time anyone in that place had ever seemed pleased with me. By then I had been shown how to change her nappy and clothes, how to lay her on alternate sides after feeding, which I might say took forever, and then you had to wind them half way through and they had to burp or they would not want any more milk. If they went to sleep while feeding we were told to flick the bottoms of their feet until they woke up, then finally you had to wind them when they had finished feeding before you laid them down or they might choke on vomit when they burped.

Now I was just turned sixteen and I took all this advice, well-meaning as it was, quite literally. So I spent ages trying to get her to burp and I didn't know what to do if she didn't, and when I got home I was on my own from the start. I would spend hours trying to get her wind up, and her back must have been getting so sore, my hand was sore from all the rubbing. Then one day my mother-in-law came to see us and noticed how long it was taking me to feed her, and she told me just to keep on feeding her and try again later, and if she didn't burp to lay her down. If she was uncomfortable with trapped wind she would cry, and when I picked her up the wind would probably come up. As easy as that! After two weeks of struggling I was amazed, the woman was a genius. Now feeding times were not as traumatic for either of us.

CHAPTER 5

Teenage mum

The day came for me to go home, and Mum sent Dick to pick me up. She had given him some clothes for me and Jane to come home in. Jane's fitted her OK, but mine didn't. I was horrified that I couldn't get into the blue two-piece suit that I liked so much. I had thought in my ignorance that my shape would still be the same as before. Luckily Mum had packed one of my maternity dresses as well as the suit I had asked for. Gloom came over me. I thought everything was going to be back to normal, and here I was wearing a bloody maternity dress again.

As I got Jane dressed, I could see Dick through the

glass doors waiting for me outside. I took my time dressing her, as I wanted him to look at me being a mum – I wanted him to love me and be proud of me. Needless to say, he didn't look. He seemed preoccupied with other thoughts and looked as if he was getting fed up with waiting for us.

The midwife carried Jane out of the hospital and gave her to me; Dick didn't even look at her. I got in the front of the car, which he had borrowed from his dad to collect me, with Jane all wrapped up on my knee, and he never said a word When we got home to my parents' house I carried her in and put her into the carrycot that Mum had got ready for me, and he still didn't look at her. I couldn't believe it, it was like we were not there. Then just as I laid her down he said "I have to go back to work" and left.

I was very upset by this, as my dream of playing happy families was destroyed. Mum and Dad were at work and would not be home for hours. I felt alone, frightened and lost. God, this was it, it was going to be awful. How would I cope?

And then the phone rings. Hello" I said, thinking it might be someone checking I was OK

"Is Dick there?"a guy's voice said.

"No, he left a while ago."

"Oh right" he said, I was wondering where he had got to. We were supposed to be going down to South-end for the day."

My world fell apart and I just put the phone down, I didn't know what to say. Then I got angry and cried with frustration. I couldn't even go and look for him – I was trapped. I spent the rest of the day planning what I would say to him when he came back.

When my parents came home they made a fuss of Jane and didn't ask about Dick not being there, not that I would have told them what had happened, as my Dad didn't need any more ammunition.

Late that night when my parents had gone to bed, in he sneaked. He got into his bed and again didn't look at Jane or me, and within seconds he was snoring. Now in between our beds, apart from the carrycot, there was a little wooden church with a steeple which my Dad had made a long time ago, on a small bedside table. The point of the steeple had worked its way loose over the years, revealing a four-inch nail that had held it in place. Without a second thought I pulled the steeple off and launched it at his head, and it hit him square on the forehead. I longed to see some sort of reaction from the bastard, but I guess he must have been drunk, because he just looked up for a second and then was snoring again. He did wonder why he had a deep scratch on his head the next day, and it had bled a bit too. I told him what I had done, and he didn't react – he just went out again to meet his mates. I wished I had got out of bed and pushed that nail right through his head.

Dick had had a tax rebate from work, and we had said that when the baby was born we would spend it on him or her. My auntie had given me the carrycot and Mum had bought the pram, but I needed to buy a larger cot for later, a highchair, bath, bedding, clothes, more nappies and so on. We had been so pleased with the £80 he had got –that was quite a lot in 1967 and would buy everything we needed and more. Dick had put it into a savings account and he always carried his savings book around with him. Anyway this day I asked if we could go shopping for the things we needed at the weekend, and he said that would be OK. When Friday night came he didn't come home until very late and as usual he went straight to bed. I thought he had just been working late with his dad, as he sometimes did. The next day he said he had to go into work for the morning and he would be back in the afternoon. I felt so proud of him and made sure that my parents knew how hard he was working now.

I waited all day for him to come home. My mum and dad just said that they thought we had been going shopping for the baby things today. I couldn't let them see how upset I was, so I told them that he had said there might have been a chance of overtime so he was still at work, I just couldn't lose face now.

It was 3 am Sunday morning when he came home and sneaked into bed and he was sleeping and snoring in a minute flat. Now I had had time to think how I was going to handle this, and I had hatched a plan. When he was sound asleep, I went through his jacket pockets to try and find a clue as to what he was up to. I found it, in the form of his little red savings book, with a balance of two pounds and a load of betting slips. He had gambled away almost the entire tax rebate. You would expect me to be angry, but I was broken-hearted and just started to sob and sob. How could he have done this to us? That money had been for our daughter. No sixteen-year-old should have to feel that much pain and anguish.

The next day he went to see his parents just to stay out of the way. I knew that if I told my dad what he had done there would be a fight and I couldn't bear it. So actually nobody was told what happened to the money, and he got away with it. Mum must have worked it out, but she wouldn't have approached me about it as she knew how defensive I was around Dick. I didn't want them to see how unhappy I was I needed to make this work so that they would be proud of me. Mum bought some of the things I needed and Dick's dad bought a second-hand cot and a pushchair. I felt as if I was in hell. It was a good job Jane was a good baby or I don't know how I would have coped, it was like sitting on a time bomb.

Dick didn't realize the terrible temper my dad had, and I was waiting for him to kill Dick. He only went to work when he felt like it, and when he was at home he did nothing but sleep; he took no interest in Jane or me. My brother, who was back home after his travels, told my mum that Dick had been seen in the Town Hall the night I was in labour, with his mates and some girls. My mum told me this years later, long after we had divorced. It didn't surprise me, but she said that James had hated him for it and for ruining my life at such a young age.

Finally the inevitable happened; there was an almighty bust-up in the kitchen. Dick was sitting at the kitchen table yawning and getting ready to go to bed at 7.30 pm, after a long day of skiving, and doing sod all, and my dad was getting ready to go to work. All I remember is my dad picking Dick up by the back of his shirt so he started to choke and pushing him against the gas cooker, holding him with one hand on his throat. He began to punch him in the face with the other. The teapot went flying, tea, tea-leaves and all, I screamed, Mum came rushing in and started to scream with me. My dad's language was foul – I had never heard him swear like that before – and my brother was standing in the doorway smiling. Something I didn't think about until after was that I never saw Dick try to defend himself. Not only had I married a liar, a cheat and a thief, he was a spineless bastard as well. Every girl's dream, huh?

The next evening we moved in with his parents down in the valley. This was a major concern to my mum, who said that taking a baby of six weeks old from the hill we lived on down into the valley at night and in the cold and dark, she could become seriously ill. This was my mum's world or la-la land as I used to call it but at the time I really believed it was a valid concern. When I get a bit neurotic some days I remind myself that it really can't be wondered at with the self-induced trauma she brought into my life – she could frighten the bejasus out of me. But I also know that she couldn't help it and she meant well. She loved Jane very much and I guess she didn't want her to go.

Jane was fine, but I kept worrying and looking for signs of sudden life-threatening illness. Dick's mum was nice enough, but I didn't like his dad much – he was always down the pub or working, one of those men who firmly believe that a meal should be on the table when they come home. He was completely bald, because he had walked into a cupboard in which there was a gas leak and lit a match to get a better look. Need I say more? There was Dick's mum blowing on his dad's soup to make sure he could eat it without having to wait for it to cool down as soon as he came in. He wasn't violent like my dad, but he was grumpy. He had a good match with his wife as she didn't like to go out or go socializing. She even had her shopping delivered, and he liked his wife to stay at home and do woman's things, so it worked. It created a quiet home, a bit too quiet for my liking but better than walking on eggshells.

Dick went to work with his dad, who was a carpenter at the local paper mill, and he went to work this time, although he would still have the odd few nights out with his mates leaving me at home. His dad didn't seem to have a problem with this but then he wouldn't, like father like son. I could tell his Mum was not OK with it, but she was so quiet and almost timid. She didn't say anything to Dick, but she did keep me company. She spent time explaining things to me, like telling me I would soon have to take Jane's dresses up as she was getting older (they were long, like baby gowns, in those days), and about teething, which I knew nothing about, what to get, what to expect, just little things, but so valuable to a young girl like me. Too many to mention, from how to clean windows to how to cook chips, most of which I carry with me to this very day. She was a wise woman, and I am grateful that she was in my life at that most awful time. No one else seemed to be.

After about two months we were offered a tied house, a house that was tied to Dick's job, just like his parents. As long as he worked at the mill we could stay in the house. It was a small two-bedroom house with a kitchen and bathroom and toilet downstairs. There was a group of four, all the same, two semis, and we were on the end next door to a pub. Like most houses in the sixties, there was no central heating and no hot water, except from a gas boiler above the kitchen sink and one above the bath that dribbled out and must have taken an hour to get half a bath of water, which by then was cold. It had four open fireplaces, one in each room, although we never lit the bedroom ones, we could never afford it. It took most of our money to feed the gas and electricity meters, sixpence for the gas and a shilling for the electric, and that might last a day or two.

I must say that Dick's dad did help. He built us some kitchen cupboards which went from floor to ceiling and more for under the sink. He asked me what colour I wanted them painted and I said tangerine would be lovely, as it was all the fashion then. I thought they looked great. Then he decorated the front room with blue and green wallpaper along with some Wedgewood blue paint I had chosen, and he also made a long sideboard for us. He really was good at his job and also a perfectionist.

In the dining room he built a cupboard in the

corner for the television to stand on, and finally he and Dick's mum bought and laid some parquet-effect lino for us. My mum and dad bought us a three-piece suite in orange with wooden arms and legs. We hired a television and were given an old spring metal bed that woke you up every time you moved in it because the springs were so old and rusty – it came with its own old flock mattress. When I think of it today it's a wonder we didn't catch something from it or get septicemia, the times we scratched our legs on it getting in and out of the damn thing.

We lived in that house for about six months, and it was awful for me. After a few weeks Dick started staying out at the weekends. After work on Fridays he just didn't come home, and the next we saw of him was usually Sunday evening, by which time he was totally broke, having had a great time with his mates. On these weekends alone with Jane I used to hope my mum and dad would come over on Saturday afternoon to see us, which they usually did after they had finished in the shop. I never told them what was happening – they just assumed Dick was at work. I knew that at some point over the weekend the gas and electricity would run out and we would have to go to bed early, and Jane would have to have a cold bottle of milk and cold food. More often than not my parents would leave some sweetie money for Jane, maybe sixpence, and I would have to use that on the gas. At least we would have hot drinks and food then, but we still had no electricity by Saturday afternoon. It wasn't too bad during the summer months, but the winter was terrible. Sometimes I used to ask if we could come and stay the weekend as it would make a nice change for Jane. They never questioned it.

Those weekends were few and far between, so almost all the time was spent at home alone, no TV, no heat. I sometimes went next door to a very old couple in their nineties who were lovely to me. They seemed to know that I was lonely and scared in the house; they always made me welcome and offered me tea and milk or squash for Jane. There was always a roaring great fire and lots of oil lamps burning, which made the house smell of paraffin, but wow, what an atmosphere it created. Every wall was covered from top to bottom with photos, all black and white, mostly of family, all hanging by pieces of string attached to nails in the wall, no picture hooks anywhere. I never counted them, but there wasn't space, they were frame to frame and there must have been 300of them – it was amazing. The radio was always on, as they had no television. A table in the centre of the room was always semi-laid with a tin of condensed milk, sugar bowl, butter dish, salt and pepper, bread (they had had to cut all the crust off because they didn't have a tooth between them) and the cups, saucers, plates, cutlery all ready. I still think of them, that summer of '67 when I used to go and sit with them in their front garden under a huge apple tree in the sun, just them, Jane and me.

The nights were the worst. When it got really dark I would gather up Jane and put her in my bed with me, and she was so good. I think children know when they have to be good. I think she could tell that I was frightened and needed her to hold on to.

To make things even more unbearable, we had rats. I would spend hours listening to them under the floorboards gnawing and scratching and it was a nightmare. They came in from the paper mill next to us where Dick sometimes worked, if he could be bothered, with his Dad. I used to find them most days in the garden and they were huge. One day I trod on a dead one while I was hanging out Jane's nappies. I screamed and my neighbour, who was in his garden, just stared at me. I said "It's a rat, I've just stood on it", thinking he would come over and pick it up for me and get rid of it, but he just looked at me and the dripping wet nappies and turned away without a word. They were a middle-aged couple who just didn't like me. Teenage mums were not accepted and it must have stuck out like a sore thumb that in some areas I wasn't coping. But I did try. Jane always had nappies

and liners to help stop nappy rash. I did everything I
was shown, but those nappies – how the hell were you
supposed to keep them white? I found out sometime
later that you were supposed to soak them, preferably
in Napisan. After that Jane had no more grey-stained
nappies – easy when you know how.

Meal times were terrible. I didn't really know how
to cook, and it was usually beans, chips and eggs.
Sometimes I managed mashed potato and beans, and
I did make ham rolls. Jane was OK as she mainly had
baby food, but I did do her boiled eggs, which she loved
with soldiers. Pudding sometimes was Carnation
evaporated milk and a tin of fruit cocktail, but we
mostly didn't have puddings as there was never
enough money. I remember weeks when all I had to
eat was dry bread because Dick was giving me less and
less. He didn't eat at home most times but ate at his
Mum's, so he was OK. He really was a piece of work.

I had hardly any clothes, just one top that Dick's
Mum had brought me back from holiday, one jumper,
one skirt, one bra and three pairs of knickers. As I
said, Mum and Dad were very hard up at the time and
I hadn't ever worked long enough to get any decent
clothes. I coped by washing everything out in the sink
at night, wringing it as tight as I could and then
hanging it over the big old nursery guard in front of
the fire. If there was no fire then I just wore the clothes

another day until I knew I would be able to dry them, but sometimes I was so desperate for clean clothes I would iron them dry. I did this quite a few times, so in the end my white top, bra and knickers had taken on a distinctly scorched look, a bit orange to say the least. Jane had quite a few clothes so it wasn't such a problem, and Dick wasn't there enough to bother about. He was a dirty sod anyway so it didn't bother him, and I know his mum did his washing sometimes, I think to make it easier for me. She didn't know the trouble I was having with him.

I guess you might wonder where my mum was in all this, as she had always been such a worrier – simple, she didn't know because I didn't tell her. That's why sometimes I had to get myself presentable in a panic so that she didn't see the state I was in most of the time. She must have just thought I really liked the skirt and top she always saw me in, but I guess she noticed when the summer was passing and I was still wearing these lightweight clothes, which were also a bit orange by now. I knew that money was tight for them; they had a heavy mortgage and Dad's drinking had spiraled out of control. My brother had gone walkabout again, so maybe Mum didn't pick up on the situation I was in.

I don't know when she first noticed, but one day while visiting me she said "I'm going up to London with your Nan, I'll bring you back some new dresses". God, I was over the moon! I could see myself and Jane walking around holding my head up for once in some half-decent clothes, feeling so proud and grown up and coping. People would think I was married to a rich bloke. Funny how a new dress can make a girl feel.

Mum told me to come over next Saturday evening and she would have them for me. Dick was at home and I asked him if he would take me to my parents because Mum had some new clothes for me. He did, but only because he was afraid of my dad. So we got in his old car, me and Jane in the front, and off we went. I noticed that Dick didn't want to talk to me. That was nothing unusual, but he was in a really strange mood.

The dresses were lovely and there were three of them. One was light blue with white lace all across the front, one was blue with short sleeves and white cuffs and tiny white buttons down the front, and the third was navy blue with long sleeves, white collar and cuffs. I wanted to try them on straight away. I was so excited to get the dresses and I so wanted Dick to see me in them. I wanted him to really love me, and I thought the dresses might change his mind when he saw how pretty I looked in them, but he pulled me to one side and said we had to go.

I felt a rollercoaster of emotions at that moment. It was like taking a blow to the stomach. I can still remember the feeling of utter abandonment and helplessness I felt. All the excitement I had felt he had taken away in one second flat.

I thanked my mum and said we had to get back to do some jobs indoors, all lies of course. I think she was just beginning to catch on.

It was starting to get dark when we got home. The fire was still alight, so I threw some more coal on, but the mood was awful. Then without a word Dick went out of the back door, and I shouted after him "where are you going?" He didn't answer. It was like a floodgate opened –I sobbed and sobbed. I guess I thought he would stay and see me try the dresses on, I was always hoping. Suddenly I hated him with a passion. I had just realized that he would never love me or take care of me. As I sat in front of the fire with Jane on my knee, I remembered that he hadn't left me any money again, and then the lights went out.

About an hour later, still sitting by the firelight, I was thinking about both of us sleeping downstairs for the night, but knowing the rats would be closer to us, when in came my brother back from another walk about. I was so happy to see him. He wanted to know why the lights were off, and I told him everything. I said I hated Dick and needed to get away from him. James had enough money to get the lights back on, which amazed me; he was always pot-less. He was just fifteen at the time and finding my situation a bit too much to understand. The way he saw it, if he beat the hell out of Dick it would sort things out, and tempting as that sounded I knew it wasn't the answer.

We had been talking for about an hour when in came Dick – very unusual for him to come back early. I started to shake because now my brother knew everything and although he was mainly a gentle guy and it took a lot for him to lose it, I knew he had waited a long time for this moment just to have a go. Dick asked him what he was doing there and James said "I've come to see my sister, is that a problem?" Dick told him to go and said he was not welcome, and James grabbed his arm. I screamed and James said "later, I'll have you later". He looked at me and asked if I would be OK and I said "Yes, but please don't tell Mum and Dad." He glanced at me, shook his head and left, while I was crying and pleading with Dick not to send him home as it was so late and I knew he would have to lie in a field or a shop doorway all night, but basically Dick didn't give a shit.

Dick said, "I saw him coming down the road and waited to see if he was coming in here". I didn't see a problem with it, but he said "I don't want him in here again". Thinking back, it was because he didn't want my brother to know how he treated me, as he knew it would get back to my Dad. So my bit of happiness that evening with my brother had gone, but I thought at least Dick had come home tonight.

When Dick was satisfied I was alone he went out, and the next time I saw him was Monday evening, when he came home, ignored me and Jane as usual and went straight to bed.

I really do not know how I got through this every day. I think it was the fact that I didn't want to let my parents see I was failing; I was always looking for their approval.

One day a friend of mine asked me if I could go to the local fair with her. It was quite an event – it came every year and they closed the high street off for three days. I hadn't been for a couple of years and was longing to get out and I loved funfairs, so I started working on my mum to look after Jane for the night. I had to do that every time I wanted to go out – it wasn't because she didn't want to look after Jane, she just didn't want me to go out, and especially going out and having fun.

So the first Saturday I saw her I asked if it would be OK if I went out with my friend to the fair. She asked me why I wasn't going with Dick (who at that time I hadn't seen for three days)and I said I was going with him as well and his friends. She agreed, so the following Friday Dad picked Jane up from me and I scurried around getting ready. My friend's brother was going to pick me up and take us both to the fair. I had two shillings and sixpence on me.

The fair was brilliant. I loved it, because I could act all of my sixteen years for the evening and forget about being a mum and a part-time wife. I did realize that night what a terrible mistake I had made marrying Dick. Seeing girls of my own age having fun and no real worries in their lives, I was jealous. I knew I had no choice but to go back home after this, and it kept taking the edge off it for me.

Just as we were getting ready to leave at about eleven I saw Dick – he was with his mates and drunk out of his head. I went up to speak to him, but he was being supported by two blokes because he couldn't even stand up, so I left and a cousin who I had met at the fair gave me a lift home. I got in and went straight up to bed. I couldn't believe it. My dressing table and wardrobe that my Dad had painted lilac and white for me had gone. The bastard had sold it that night between me going out and coming home. No wonder he had been steaming drunk, he had had money to do it.

I fell asleep, crying and wondering what I was going to tell my Dad. Then the light came on and I heard a guy say, "Oh sorry, Dick said there was no one home." I sat bolt upright. I knew it was Dick's best mate.

"Where is he?" I said.

"Down stairs on the sofa" his mate said.

I went downstairs to face six guys in my sitting room, all half cut, and found they had taken out my kitchen window to get in because prat face had lost his keys and was now merrily chucking up all over the parquet-effect lino. They left quickly after saying sorry for the hole where the window used to be. I went to bed.

The next morning I began cleaning the floor; he was still asleep and probably wouldn't have done it anyway. It was very early as I had to be at my mum's by eight to pick up Jane so she could get to work. I went upstairs to get dressed and then heard him coming up. He was all over me saying how sorry he was, he would change, he loved me and he would come with me to fetch Jane home. To be honest, although in my heart I knew he didn't mean any of it, for me it was a way out of having to explain to my parents what he had done and we could carry on as if nothing had happened, so I forgave him. Pig.

He did become a bit more reliable for a while after that. He wasn't having as many weekends out and we even managed to save a bit of money each week. So most Saturdays we would go into town and buy a few bits for the house and I was feeling so much better. I was far from happy, but I was feeling more secure.

One day Dick came home and said that there was

another house available to rent a bit nearer to the mill and newer, and it didn't come with resident rats. We moved in the next week. It was a lovely chalet-type house with three large bedrooms, bathroom, two toilets, a huge kitchen and a through lounge and dining room. Mum helped me get some curtains, which were mainly hers and Nan's old ones. They were awful, a kind of green tartan – I don't know what it was with my mum and tartan. We didn't have any curtain rails, so I tried hanging them on net curtain wire. They were far too heavy for that, so they sagged in the middle when they were drawn together. They did cover the window, but god they did look awful.

Dick decided to get the stairs and living room measured for carpets, so we chose old gold for the stairs hall and landing, a rich yellow colour, and bright red for the living room. Of course within a few weeks the old gold looked more like old mould – it was filthy. But you live and learn, and I was growing up fast.

The neighbours were all very nice and mostly Scottish, like Dick. That's when we began having parties. All Dick's mates would come, my brother and his friends – yes, Dick and James had decided to get on and James was staying with us most of the time by then, and the neighbour, who were about our age. It was a good time. I never used to drink – it was all about enjoying the music, company and dancing, which I loved. I had been so unhappy and now I could let off some steam. I really needed that. I even got a shared job with my neighbour at the paper mill. I did mornings while she looked after Jane, and she did afternoons while I had her two children. It worked really well, and the extra money was handy.

I thought at that time there was hope for us and that we would stay together, but it didn't last. Dick went back to his old ways again and wasn't getting up for work. His dad used to come round some mornings to see what was up and why he hadn't turned up. He would just shout upstairs "Get up, Dick!" and then go away. Sometimes he would get up, but mostly he didn't.

One morning when his dad came around I didn't want to let him in. I had been trying to get Dick up for ages and I had lost my temper and started shouting at him. He told me to shut up and said he would do what he liked and that he had had enough and was going out. As he got out of bed and went downstairs I picked up a really heavy ornament and launched it at the back of his head. It missed and went flying into the wall and smashed to bits. He didn't even flinch – I swear he was dead from the neck up. Anyway there was now quite a large hole in the wall and a mess all over the floor, so it was obvious what had happened. I didn't want anyone to know what was going on and I certainly didn't want my father-in-law to see, but I had to let him in. He looked at the mess and then at me. "He wouldn't get up again," I said in my defence. He looked away and said "Are you all right son?" then went and joined him in the kitchen. I don't know what was said, but Dick got dressed and left with his Dad to go to work with not a backward glance at me. He didn't come home that night but stayed at his parents. I guess that was the beginning of the end.

Just before the final split came my brother, Dick and I were sitting watching TV one Saturday afternoon when Dick said something to James about our mum always interfering, which she never did –in fact I wish she had been interfering, maybe things wouldn't have got so out of control. Now my brother was very placid and I didn't expect him to react in such a violent way, and Dick didn't see it coming either. James jumped up out of his chair and Dick jumped up out of his and began to run. He had made it through the front door out onto the drive when James got him. We had an old wooden shed on the drive and by the time I had got outside my brother was holding him up against the shed by his throat with one hand and punching him in the face with the other. He was a lot bigger than Dick and now his moment had come, he had waited for this for a long time.

Neither of us was violent by nature, but I decided

to join in– my time had come too. I started to throw as many stones as I could at him without hitting my brother and all you could hear was the sound of thumps, slaps and bangs. Dick was bleeding when it was over. My brother let go of him and he fell to the ground. We looked at each other and grinned, then went back inside, shut the door and left him there. He was only there for a few seconds and then he got up and went skulking off to his parents. It was over.

James went home and told Mum and Dad what had happened, and my dad was delighted. That evening he came over to see me. He didn't ask any questions, only asked if I wanted to come home. I said yes, so he put us in the car along with our few clothes and took us home with him. That's why I loved him. We settled in as if we had never been away and Jane thrived – she loved the attention and the fuss they made of her.

She slept in with me for the first few days until we arranged with the manager of the mill to meet at the house one evening to let us in so that we could get Jane's cot, high chair, push chair, and toys. It was quite dark and we met him outside the back door. He told us that Dick had not been there for a week or so nor at work, so he needed to get the things moved out anyway. He was so nice and seemed really concerned about me and Jane.

He let us in and switched on the kitchen light, and guess who was waiting in the shadows – Dick's Dad. Someone at work had obviously told him what was going to happen, and as his spineless son couldn't face us, he did.

"Everything in this house belongs to my son," he said. "He bought it, so it's his."

I began to shake. I thought there was going to be a punch up. None of us could believe it. Even his own granddaughter's cot he wouldn't let us take.

I could see that the mill manager was amazed by all of it and he said to Dick's dad, "I'll see you in the morning Bill". My dad was really calm, not what I had expected, but I think he got a lot of satisfaction by letting Bill show his true colours in front of his employer.

The manager was very concerned about what had happened and said that if there was anything he could do to help, just to let him know. I know Bill heard this as he was shutting the door on us. He did lose his job soon after and the lot of them moved back to Scotland.

My parents had to buy everything again for Jane, and they never got over the fact that he had got away with it. As the law stood in those days the main breadwinner, who was nearly always the man, got to keep everything because he had paid for it. In this case of course he hadn't, but if you had no receipts to prove it you were stuffed. Thank God the law was updated later. I had my parents to fall back on, but some girls didn't, which was why they stayed with such utter arse holes, as they had no way out.

Thing was, I was three months pregnant and my parents didn't know. Mum eventually realized and she was fine about it, and so was Dad, although they were worried about the space in their two-bedroom bungalow. They gave me the small bedroom and Jane and I slept in the double bed, and the cot was ready for the baby at the end of the bed. Mum had said I needed to get put on the council waiting list, which I did, but I was told there would be a seven-year wait, because as my parents had taken us in and we had a room for ourselves we were not classed as urgent. I can tell you that was such a relief to hear. I really didn't want to be on my own again, especially with a new baby.

My parents were fine about it – I think secretly they wanted the children living with them; it gave them something to do in the evenings. More so for my mum. She and Dad didn't hold conversations and they didn't have a social life. She used to say that the only time he ever spoke to her was to ask for a cup of tea. So all in all we got on fine, and I was quite happy to take a back seat for a while and let them take over with Jane.

When I was about eight months pregnant, I went

to court for maintenance for Jane and the baby. Dick turned up with a list as long as your arm telling of debts for things he had bought during our brief marriage. It was all lies – except for the carpets he had had bought, there were no other debts. The thing was, I had to hand it to him, he was very well presented and very well spoken, obviously intelligent, plausible, and a very good liar. They fell for it all. I never got a chance to speak. My very young and very useless solicitor did all that for me. I did warn him about Dick's charms but he wasn't prepared for it. Dick, who represented himself, wiped the floor with him, and had an answer for everything. He made me look as if I hadn't been able to cope and was no good as a wife or mother and that I had run back home to my parents at every opportunity.

My dad was sitting next to me and I could feel the tension coming of off him, but he managed to keep calm. The judge awarded Jane ten shillings a week and the baby two shillings and sixpence, and told Dick that he had to leave the money at the court every week. I couldn't believe he had got away so lightly.

Dick left the court room quickly, and I was grateful for that, as I knew my dad had wanted to get hold of him, but there was no sign of him outside the court. Dad said "so that's all this baby's worth to him, two and a kick," and that became her nickname when she was very small.

Me as a little girl with my rabbits

With James and Dad in the back yard

With the two jackdaws that came
everywhere with me

Me and James

James at the age of 18

With my lovely daughters: left to right, Louise, me,
Lucy and Catherine

As it turned out Dick never paid a penny. He went and lived in Jersey, where the law is different and no one could touch him. He never remembered their birthdays or Christmas, and it was as if they had never existed for him.

On Friday January 23 1970 we were all watching Michael Miles and "Take Your Pick" and Jane was still up – she had no real routine and mostly went to bed when I did. She was a real live wire and needed very little sleep, so letting her stay up late was a way of sometimes getting a lie-in. She asked to go to bed, so we said goodnight and went up. Seconds later my waters broke and she jumped out of bed shouting "Sue's wet the bed!" In rushes Mum, just as I'm getting up to go to the loo before any more water gushes out.

I passed my dad in the hall. "All right then?" he said. "Yes" I said, but I wasn't, I was shaking like a leaf. I sat on the loo and Dad phoned an ambulance. I stayed there until they came to take me to the maternity home, as I felt so uncomfortable about my parents seeing me like that.

The paramedics knocked on the bathroom door and I opened it, and to my horror they had brought in a wheelchair. My mum had put a big thick towel on the seat. It was another "God kill me now" moment. I was still so young, and anyone but my parents would have been better.

I said, "Do I have to sit in that thing?"

"It would be easier if you did," said the paramedic, who looked older than my dad. When I thought about it, it would be worse with water running down my legs on the way to the ambulance with Mum and Dad walking behind me in the wet trail I was leaving. It didn't bear thinking about, so I got in the wheelchair, and thanked God it was dark. 'Silent labour' was what the midwife called it; I was having regular contractions without the pain.

It was a pushover compared to the last time. I was in the delivery room from when I first got into the hospital, and as I lay there feeling very calm and thinking "maybe this is how it is with your second baby," the pain started and it was full-on labour no gradual build up. I was almost ready to have the baby, and at 5.35 am Saturday she was born.

My Louise. Six pounds eleven ounces, and like a little red ball with masses of black hair. Unlike her sister, she screamed the moment she came into the world. We were only in the maternity home for 24 hours and they let us go home. Things had moved on so much since I had had Jane three years earlier, thank God. Jane was really good with her, she was never jealous, and Louise was a happy baby and so much more laid back than Jane, which made for an easier life this time, and with the support of my parents, we all got along fine.

When Louise was six weeks old my brother returned from another walkabout and soon after he met Stella, the girl he would marry. I got on well with her, and not long after they had met we found she was pregnant. They were married and went to live in a council house quite away from us. I think everything was OK, until they had another baby —maybe it was the pressure on them, I don't know, but this is about my life, not my brother's and I don't feel it would be fair to talk about his life at that time. All I know is that he wasn't getting on too well at home, and I think he would frequently go off as he had always used to. I knew from the start that marriage would be a big mistake for him being such a free spirit.

In my own life around that time I had met a man. Louise was ten months old, and as I didn't go out socializing I might never have met anyone again for years, but he kind of came to me. Joe was our ice cream man, and I got to know him over one summer buying ice cream every day for Jane. We used to make small talk at his van and he had started stopping outside my house waiting for us to go out. He was extremely handsome, three years older than me and seemed like a really nice guy.

It was a very gradual thing, but towards the end of the summer he asked me out. At first I said no as I didn't think my parents would approve of me going out with the ice cream man. I think I must have offended him because I didn't see him for about five weeks, and that really upset me as I had grown fond of him. Then one day in November I heard his jingle playing and went out and there he was waiting for me. I said I would like to go on a date with him but not for the next two weeks, as I knew I would have to work on my Mum. He was fine with that. It was the start of a long relationship that would last almost five years.

Life with Mum and Dad was to say the least busy. Mum was at work all day and Dad was either at home in bed during the day or at work. When he was on night work it was a nightmare trying to keep the girls busy without making a noise, especially in the winter when we were stuck in. We lived about four or five miles from the town and the buses were not reliable, and it cost so much to get one anyway that most of the time we just stayed in the house or the garden if it was nice. James had now married Stella and they had a baby boy. They were living with her parents and looking to get a place of their own. Joe and I had been going out together for about six months when he bought and renovated an old house that he had intended to rent. He knew my brother and Stella were looking for a place, so he let them move in.

Joe and I were very much a couple, and he loved

the girls. He always took notice of them, bought them little toys, and always asked about them if he didn't see them for a couple of days. Gradually as the months went on he would call around to my parents' house every night after work and we would all sit around and talk, something my mum and dad had never done, but Joe seemed to bring out the best in them; he was full of life and very ambitious, something my Dad liked in him. Funny, I never heard my dad say one negative thing about him in all the time he knew him. Maybe Dad thought this man would be a good husband for me and it would take some of the pressure off him, I don't know. Dad liked independent people and Joe certainly was one of those. He had bought his first property at the age of twenty, and he was on his way to buying his next.

One thing my dad didn't know about Joe, thank God, was that he was very passionate. For three months I tried to keep him at arm's length, as I was so terrified of getting pregnant again, but in the end I gave in (willingly, I might add). We made an appointment with the family planning clinic and I went on the pill. It's a part of your child's life that most parents can't accept, although they know it's happening. I go cold when I think of the risks we took in my parents' house, having no place of our own to go, and me always at home at night indoors with the girls.

We would wait until Mum and Dad went to bed, give it half an hour and then push the sofa against the living room door, so that if anyone wanted to come in they couldn't without knocking on the door first. We hadn't thought about my dad knocking on the door of his own living room, what would I have said? "Oh all right Dad, hang on, I'll just push the sofa out of the way and get some clothes on." Were we really that stupid? I think they probably knew what was happening when they went to bed, but none of us wanted to think it.

Sometimes we went into the conservatory if it wasn't too cold. We needed to be together, and we had a passion for each other like nothing I had known before. We were always saying how much we loved each other, and out of this developed a really deep friendship. We did everything together and he never once minded the girls always being there; he treated them as his own, and could never understand why their dad had no contact with them. I didn't know he had moved to Jersey then.

Only after a couple of years did my insecurity start to raise its head. I had asked Joe about his family, but he never wanted to talk about them. I knew they were in Italy, while he was living with his brother and sister-in-law over here. I didn't understand why I hadn't met them; after all, he knew my family well by then. I kept on, so he had to tell me in the end. They didn't know about me – he said they would never accept a divorced woman into the family. I was so angry and upset. Same old story Sue, I thought, you're still not good enough. I almost blew the relationship out of the water there and then, but he was devastated. He told me he knew this was how I would react and that was why he had kept quiet. He didn't want to risk losing me; he would rather lose his family.

I felt that no one could love me this much, and I began to distrust him. I started phoning him at work and would become so upset that he would have to leave and come and talk to me. His main job was as a chef so it wasn't easy for him to just walk out, but he did as much as he could. He kept saying "I love you Susie, I would never hurt you". I knew it was in my head, but I just couldn't help myself. I had been on cloud nine for so long I knew it would have to end.

He bought me a dog and a cat and Mum and Dad were fine about it; it was understood that they would be coming with us when we moved out, but they didn't know I was having second thoughts about that.

He took me to his solicitor and got me my divorce, and he took me and the girls all over England looking for a property that would be our home. He did try, and he never gave up on me. I told Mum, but she wasn't very happy about the idea, I don't know why. I like to think it was because she wanted more for me, like a proper wedding, but I think it was more that she didn't want me to take Jane and Louise away, as they had become such a real part of her life, and I know she would have dreaded being on her own with just Dad for company. Dad was fine about it as he trusted Joe.

Eventually we found somewhere, in Lancashire, a fish and chip shop with a three-bedroom property above it. It was so far away, but it was cheap to buy and Joe said five years and we would be able to afford to move back. We went to his solicitors to purchase the business. Joe had ten thousand pounds in cash in a biscuit tin that was thick with dust from all the months under his bed (he didn't like banks). The solicitor sat and counted the lot, and it was done. And I still wasn't sure. I really didn't believe right up to the last minute that this was ever going to happen. The thing that swayed me was that he told his brother all about me and my girls and he accepted it. He had no choice really, as Joe would have turned his back on them.

The night before I moved out of my parents' home, Joe and I went for a drive. It was the middle of January 1973, just about two weeks before Louise's third birthday, it was snowing, and I had had an attack of nerves. We went for a drink and then parked up outside the village hall to make some final arrangements before he went home for the night. I told him I couldn't go through with the move as it was so far away. He just stared at me. "Why didn't you say before now?" he said.

"I told you I didn't think it would get this far," I said.

I felt like I had betrayed him. I asked him to take me home, but he insisted on talking about it. After almost three hours, almost at midnight, we reached an agreement. I would go with him as planned, but it was to just to see how things went, and if the girls or I were unhappy he would bring us home. Now I felt so much better, as I could look upon this as an adventure, a bit like a holiday. Of course I couldn't tell Mum or Dad – all this upheaval and I might come home again – but I knew they wouldn't mind if I did.

Joe took me home, kissed me goodnight and said, "See you at eight". I was up at six; my cousin had brought a van for some of the things I was taking. The girls were staying behind with Mum and Dad for a week until we had settled in. I hated leaving; I had never been away from them before.

My poor mum would have to walk Jane to school before she got two buses to work with Louise in all that freezing weather, work from nine till two, get two buses home, walk and get Jane from school at three, go shopping, get their tea and Dad's, then bath, supper and bed. She must have had to get up at five to do all this. I never really gave that a thought till now. How selfish young people can be. It really is all about them most of the time, and she never complained about it once.

That's why I loved her.

CHAPTER 6

A cold Christmas

We arrived in Lancashire that afternoon, and it was snowing and freezing cold. The house smelled of fish and stale cooking oil and was as cold inside as outside. It hit me then that I had made a mistake; I had known before I left my parents, but it had all spiralled out of control. I wanted to turn right around and run back home.

I phoned Mum later that night to check on the girls and to tell her everything was fine. I couldn't tell her the truth, because I had to give this a go. After talking to the girls and saying goodnight to them I put the phone down, went upstairs, shut myself in the bathroom and sobbed. Joe was busy, so he didn't notice.

Then I heard a knock on the door downstairs and Joe called me. All puffy-eyed, I went to see what he wanted and at the door stood a very round and smiling lady who took my hand and welcomed me to the street. She was our next-door neighbour June, and she was lovely. She said she knew we were moving in today so she had made tea and sandwiches for us, so would we come next door and meet the family.

This was my first experience with a northerner (apart from Dad) and I loved it. Everyone I met was so friendly to me. In fact I made more friends up there in six months than in all my life down south. It was that kindness that got me through some of the worst times up there in that shop, so far from home.

A week later Mum and Dad brought the girls up on the train. It was snowing heavily and some of the trains were being delayed. When they arrived it was just a quick hello and goodbye again, and they had to get the next train back. I was crying, the girls were crying, Mum was crying, Joe was crying (he could never help himself), and then they were gone. I stared after them, just wanting to scream "Please don't leave, take us home with you!" But instead I got the girls into the car and we took them "home".

June had two sons a little older than the girls,

lovely boys, and in true northern fashion they were best friends in no time at all. The one thing I never got used to was the way they would just walk into your house without knocking – I found that so odd. One day while I was in the bath the back door opened and a friend of mine called out "you in, Sue?" "In the bath" I said, so she came into the bathroom and carried on a full conversation with me while I sat huddled in the bath in a state of shock for about ten minutes until she said "I'll put the kettle on". They were so lovely though that I couldn't help but envy their way of life.

We settled Jane into school, while Louise was at home with me. The nearest nursery was three miles away I didn't drive and buses were now and then, so I walked. It was all hills and it nearly killed me. So we stayed home after that.

It all seemed to go wrong quickly. Basically it all revolved around money and the lack of it, for me anyway. The argument was that we had a business that needed to be built, and that we shouldn't have to buy food outside the shop – we should eat fish and chips all the time or something else deep fried. My argument was that my girls needed fresh vegetables, fruit, meat and so on, but he didn't get it. He reluctantly gave me the odd pound or two here and there, but I never had housekeeping and had to ask for everything. He even locked his till at lunchtimes and he wore the key that locked it around his waist on a chain, while the shop was closed for an hour and he was upstairs doing (or cooking) his books. If I had known how tight he was with money there would have been no way on God's earth I would have moved in with him.

I worked hard in the shop while I was there, with very little return. I served when I could and made fishcakes with my little helper Louise. I would sit her on the draining board and she would help me pick out the bones from the off cuts of fish that had been soaking in warm water to loosen them. I weighed the dried peas and soaked a bucket full of them in cold water along with a good squirt of bright green dye to make them look tastier ready for boiling the next day. Each night the shop had to be cleaned and the floor washed, and on Saturday night after closing Joe brought in from outside a big chip barrel and put it in the middle of the kitchen floor, then filled it with hot soapy water and dismantled the chip fryers. I would wash the parts as he brought them into me. Every Saturday night I used to fall into utter despair. This was no life for a young girl, and the more time went on, the more frustrated I became. At about two in the morning we would finish and go to bed. The shop wasn't open on Sundays, so he used to stay in bed till midday while I was up coping with dinner and the girls, every bit as tired as he was. I began to hate him.

I used to feel resentful of my neighbour because she had lots of mod cons, for those days. Hoover, washing machine, electric kettle, lovely furniture, carpets, beautiful curtains and lovely clothes for herself and her boys. I swept up my lino floors with a broom. I went to the launderette every other day, and our clothes were starting to fall apart.

Joe did buy me a cheap wedding ring, but it kept turning my finger green so I chucked it, and he never asked about it, although I wanted him to so I could tell him I was worth more than that, hoping to shame him. Apart from that he bought Jane a hat one day in town because I said I was cold and she needed one.

Lots of women were in situations like that in the seventies, but I had been through it before as a very young girl, and I had thought this time I had got someone who really loved me and would take care of me and the girls. How wrong I was. I was tired of feeling like an old woman and a drudge. I didn't want to tell my mum and dad that once again I had failed, so week after week I struggled on with a man I hated in a loveless relationship.

Things came to a head one day when I had to go out and asked Joe to make sure that the backdoor was left unlocked so that Jane could get in after school. We could see the school from the shop – it was just over the road, and she liked to come home with her friends. He knew she was a nervous child and she would be upset if she couldn't get in. He always locked the door when he was on his own, I suppose because of his till money.

When I got home the back door was locked, Joe was upstairs doing his books and Jane wasn't there. I shouted at him, and started to cry. As I was running out of the door with Louise in tow the phone rang; it was June saying Jane was with her. She had gone around there crying because she couldn't open the backdoor.

I didn't know what to say to June. I didn't want her to know what was happening back home so I made up some excuse about the door getting stuck.

That night when the girls were in bed I wiped the floor with him. I would have quite happily killed him, but he didn't see what all the fuss was about. It was then I realised that no one would ever love my girls like I did; I wouldn't leave either of them with him again.

Christmas was about two months away, and I had no money for presents. I didn't ask Joe because I thought he might just offer, but he didn't. So I did what most others did and ordered a catalogue and got a few things for the girls and a present each for Mum, Dad and Nan, just so they would think I was managing OK. I paid for these on a weekly basis with my Family Allowance, which was the equivalent of 99 pence a week I hated Joe so much some days. He never asked how I got the presents. He was not in the slightest bit interested – maybe he believed in Santa, the tight bastard.

On Christmas Eve he shut the shop at four and we cleaned till seven, then Joe went to bed. The girls and I hung their stockings up and went to bed excited. I just wanted to go home. I was so miserable that I hadn't been able to get them the presents they had asked for. They had a couple of little cheap toys and I didn't know what they were going to say in the morning. I think if I could have driven the car I would have left there and then and taken them home. My heart was breaking for them. What I had brought them into?

Christmas morning came and they were up early unwrapping their presents. They did seem rather quiet, but they seemed happy enough. I told them Santa hadn't been able to bring all their presents, but he was going to try and get them the things they had asked for and come back another time.

Joe made an appearance three hours later. He got his coffee, put the TV on and never said a word to me or the girls. We had no Christmas tree, no decorations not even a proper Christmas dinner. Italians do it different from us, but we didn't even have an Italian-style Christmas – we had chicken with potatoes and mushy peas. There were no presents from him to me or the girls and nothing from us to him. We did have booze but I didn't drink then, and maybe it was just as well or I might have just committed murder that Christmas Day.

We got through the day and I spoke to Mum and Dad on the phone, wishing them a merry Christmas and holding back the tears. They spoke to the girls and said they would be up soon to bring them their Christmas presents, and that really cheered them up.

After that awful Christmas, the shop opened and it all got back to normal. But things were not normal, in any sense of the word. Joe and I didn't talk much any more and he said that he was going to put the shop on the market and sell up. We didn't talk about what was going to happen between us, but I think we both knew it was over.

I couldn't think too much about it. If we split up I would have to go home to my parents and admit to another failed relationship. I didn't want to think about it, although I knew it was inevitable. Part of me felt afraid and another part of me felt excited to think that this might be my way out.

One day in March my little helper and I were

boning fish for Joe to make his fish cakes and she was sitting on the draining board next to me with a towel under her to stop her getting cold (no central heating then, and it was always freezing in the kitchen). We both had our coats on and she looked at me, and her eyes seemed so sad. I said to her, "When you and Mummy have finished doing this fish I'll take you to the park". She smiled, and I thought that's all she needs in her little life to make her happy, and here she is with her little hands freezing – what I have done? I lifted her down and told her to go upstairs and play for a while, and I would come and get her and we would go to the park. When she was upstairs I picked up the bowl of stinking fish and launched it at the kitchen wall.

When I came back from the park I picked up the phone and spoke to Mum. I told her Joe was selling the shop and said could I come home? Of course she said yes, so I was done.

When I told Joe I was leaving him, he immediately changed. So nice, begging and pleading with me not to go, telling me things would be different, but I told him it was all too late. My mind was made up; we were going home.

Those last four weeks packing and getting ready to go were the happiest I had been in Lancashire. At Easter weekend my parents came to fetch us home. I was so glad to see them, and so were the girls. We loaded up Dad's car. The girls didn't bother to say goodbye to Joe, and I didn't make them. Mum got in the car and said, "Go and talk to Joe, he's crying into a tea towel". I said, "I've already said goodbye Mum, he will be OK".

Until that moment I don't think Mum had realised that it might be over between Joe and me. I think she just thought I would be staying with them until we got somewhere else to buy. God, did I feel awful! I hadn't thought to say we were coming home for good. She just stared at me and I gulped.

At the end of the day I had failed again, or that was how I saw it. I had just given five years of my life to a prick. It took me many years to understand that it was not all my fault. Anyway I knew at that moment that I was coming home for good, and I don't think she minded – she just had to pretend to.

CHAPTER 7

Leaving the nest

We settled in back home as though we had never been away. Jane's new northern accent disappeared after a couple of weeks back at her old school and the girls were so happy to be back with Mum and Dad again. I know Mum was happy, although she never said as much.

After about two months, Joe came to see us. He had sold the shop and was going to America to visit his brother. We talked that evening about the future and he said when he came home in about six months' time we should try again to make it work between us. He had realised that he had been wrong about not giving me any money for things and promised that it would be different next time. I kind of believed him, and he had been such a big part of my life, but I knew in my heart it would never be the same again. So I waved him off on a sunny morning in June 1975 and never saw him again.

I was always busy with the girls. I always tried my hardest to keep them looking nice. I didn't have an income as such, so new clothes were a luxury I could never really afford. I sewed and I was good at it and enjoyed it, so almost everything the girls wore had been sewn or knitted for them. When they were in bed at night I would set up my sewing machine and sew till two or three in the morning most nights. My dad used to say that all I needed was my girls, and he was right, they were my world. I hardly went out at all, but whenever a girlfriend phoned and asked me to go with her to a party or something it was the same old story, it would take me at least a couple of weeks of working on my mum before she would let me out, even though I was 25 years old. I don't know why she was like that with me. I always felt that because she never went out socially and never had, because she believed you should stay at home when you have children, I had to be the same. "You have children now Susanne, so you no longer have a life" she said, and that how she was. But sooner or later she would crack. Maybe it was guilt, I don't know, but I got out maybe half a dozen times a year. I did have a curfew, at midnight, and if I wasn't in by then she would be waiting for me, accusing me of having low moral standards and having been up to no good, as if coming in late meant promiscuity and coming in early meant innocence. I couldn't work her out sometimes, so it just wasn't worth the hassle– I made sure I was home by midnight.

My dad had been a tyrant in his earlier years, but he was much more easy-going now about me going out, and if I could have trusted him to have the girls on his own I could have gone out every night – he just wasn't that bothered. Not going out didn't bother me too much, as I liked to be at home. Looking back now, I feel I was a bit of a recluse. I had zero confidence and I felt old and unattractive. I guess I had just settled for my lot in life. I was secure, the girls were loved and wanted, and I didn't really have any money worries. I was also very immature. My world up to then had been very small and I had no people skills and no social skills, and was painfully shy. I had never really worked at a job or career and had never been abroad or travelled. I struggled making friends, so I just didn't try. I think I lived in a kind of unreal world, but I was safe.

One of the first things we did when we came home

SUSANNE DEFOE

was to go and see my brother and his wife. Mum had always said everything was fine with them whenever I asked, but I hadn't seen them for over a year. James wasn't there, just Stella and the two children. Mum had to tell me that they had been having a few problems in the marriage and they didn't know where my brother was, but she hadn't wanted to worry me. My sister-in law wasn't in such good health, so we took her and the children home with us. God knows how we managed in a two-bedroom bungalow.I think my parents were brilliant, they gave up their bedroom for them and slept in the sitting room on a couple of fold-up beds. They were almost different people from the ones who had brought me up. My dad had definitely mellowed and had stopped drinking at home. He was always a good grandfather and seemed to cope better with his grandchildren – he had a lot more patience and time for them. Mum as usual was always worrying about them, but she absolutely doted on them. I asked someone why this might be, and they said that parents don't usually have such high expectations of their grandchildren as have with their own children, so it didn't matter so much what they did. Whether it was that I don't know, never will, but you couldn't fault them as grandparents.

James did come home again, he always did, and they all went back home, for a while anyway. They were still having problems – he kept leaving and Stella and the kids kept coming back to Mum and Dad's. Then she was pregnant again, and of course nothing changed, it just seemed to get worse. I know there was a lot that went on in their marriage that I never knew about at the time, and will never know, and I guess that's for the best.

Because of complications during her pregnancy, Stella had to have a hysterectomy when the baby was six weeks old, so her three children were left with me. In my bedroom I had Jane in the top bunk, Louise in the bottom bunk, my brother's two eldest in bed with me and the baby in her pram, which was pushed up against the only remaining wall in the bedroom. Mum and Dad were in their own room and James was on the sofa. I did get into a routine after a few weeks, but it was difficult with my dad on night work every two weeks. When it was raining it was a nightmare trying to keep them quiet. Dad still had a temper and a couple of doors had holes in them where he had thrown the alarm clock at them or put his fist through them. I couldn't do much about it; I just used to breathe a sigh of relief when he left at 7.30 pm to go to work.

I had a large cardboard box full of toys and games that came out whenever we were stuck indoors. The room was strewn with them until just before Mum came in, when they were chucked back in the box. I think the kids were as sick of those toys as me, but without money or a car I couldn't get very far with five of them and I used to dread rainy days.

I did manage to get my nephew into school with Jane and Louise. He was just about old enough, so they took him in for a while – I think they felt sorry for me. When I remember that walk to the school twice a day, pushing a pram with my six-week-old niece in it, my two-year-old niece balanced on top of the pram, two five-year-olds holding onto either side of the pram and Jane holding on to me, I remember thinking "I hope to god people don't think these kids are all mine!"

Mornings were absolute chaos. I was still feeding the baby through the night and I felt exhausted. After getting them up, fed, washed and dressed, we would set off for school, which was about a twenty-minute walk. One blessing was that it was summer and they could go into the garden after school, which meant less risk of holes in the doors. I had lots of outdoors toys, swing, slide, seesaw, large rocking horse, a pool with lots of floaty things in it. I had acquired most of it with the help of Joe some time ago and thousands of Green Shield Stamps. He had been collecting them for years and had never bothered to stick them in the books, so he gave them to me. It must have taken a month of licking and sticking, my tongue was sore and I had cut my lips several times, but I got there in the end. I got a catalogue and ordered the toys for the garden. I can't remember how many books of stamps I had in the end I just remember sitting there every night surrounded by bloody Green Shield Stamps. So I guess I got something from the five years I was with him.

Night times were never as bad as the mornings. Mum was home by then, and they all had dinner at about six, then bathed two at a time, then drinks and supper, story time, then sleep by 8.30 if I was lucky. They were all pretty good and hardly ever had fights, considering they were so confined. It worked well and I got into the swing of it, but I must say I wouldn't have wanted to do it for long.

Stella left hospital four weeks later and because there was quite a long recovery after a hysterectomy she had been advised to only take one child home at a time so that she didn't overdo it. So she took one the first week, another the next week and finally the baby went home. Ah bliss, the house seemed so empty and quiet, but I missed them.

I was just getting back to life with my own two children when my brother called to say that Stella had had to go back to hospital with complications. After that she never seemed well and was back and forth to the hospital for the next two years. I figured this was how my life would be now. I felt like a drudge, and began to hate my brother, who was never around much. I had his children most of the time and when he was there he never took any notice of them, or anyone for that matter. Although his music had always been such a big part of his life, he had stopped playing his guitar. He began to blame Stella. I thought most of the blame should lie at her feet as she was always feeling unwell and unable to cope, but what about me? I had to cope regardless of how I felt. I felt she was pulling my brother down with her, and it always came back to me: "Sue will have them". They never asked, not even my mum. I was always at home, so I was the obvious choice. I was tired and angry and felt about forty years old. I had tried so hard to be reasonable, and to do what they wanted me to do without making too much of a fuss, but now I had reached my limit. I didn't think it would ever end. I can still remember the frustration I felt, and the feeling of being totally trapped with nowhere to run and hide from it all.

Mum had bought a second-hand car to learn to drive and I was teaching her most evenings. I had passed my test sometime before and had longed to get a car and some much-needed freedom, but I could never afford it. I did borrow Dad's Ford Capri once – he was a bit reluctant to lend it me, but he did, just told me to be careful. That evening coming back from my friend's house I pulled onto Dad's drive and took a very large brick pillar that was attached to the metal gate with me. The long front of Dad's shiny black car was half the length it had been. I thought he would go mad at me, but all I heard him say was "bloody hellfire!" He got in, it reversed it and drove it back onto the drive, driving over a pile of bricks and rubble and a twisted metal gate, then went indoors and never mentioned it again. He booked the car into the garage the next day and had it repaired within a week and it was looking like new again. He never let me borrow it again. I would have thought that someone with my Dad's temper would have flipped, but he was so calm. Again it seemed it was the little things in life that drove him crazy.

My brother and I had never fallen out since we were kids. We got on well, but now I didn't know him any more. I didn't know what was wrong. As child i had lead such a sheltered life I wasn't in the least bit street wise. I had never been to night clubs, didn't drink or do drugs. If I had been a little more worldly-wise, maybe I would have guessed that he was into hard drugs. It wasn't until a few years later that I was told this, so life just went on as normal, but the strain on my Mum was showing. There were sometimes ten of us in my parents' two-bedroom bungalow. James and Stella had to move out of their rented house as it was going to be sold, and they were housed by the council. But they were hardly ever there.

Mum said it was time I had my own place and said she was going to get in touch with the council about it. This was in 1976.I had lived with them almost all my life and it came as a bit of a shock. I think I thought I would be there forever, and now she wanted me gone. I didn't want to go anywhere. We were OK where we were, with them, but she was determined. I began to think she was getting me out of the way so that she had more room for Stella and James – maybe she was, I'll never know. Although I loved my brother very much I had always been slightly jealous of him, and Mum always seemed to have more time for him. He was aware of it and he tried not to let her fuss him too much in front of me.

Just before my parents were taking their annual holiday in July with the girls and me in tow, I received a letter from the local council saying I had been given a three-bedroom house on the other side of town, about eight miles from Mum, and that it was new and ready for me to move in next week. Oh God – it was going to happen! I would have to cope all on my own from now on. Mum was pleased and Dad took us to see the house before we went on holiday. It was nice, with large patio doors, under-floor heating and a large bathroom, but I didn't want it. I had to sound enthusiastic about it though, or my poor mum would have thought she would never get rid of us and I didn't want her to think

I was weak in any way. I have always tried to come across as a strong person with a devil-may-care attitude, so I think she would have been very surprised to learn just how frightened I was.

So I just went along with it. We had our holiday on the Isle of Wight and when we got home I started to try and get a few bit and pieces together for our new home. My parents helped of course, with a bed for me a cooker and curtains. Anyway I started to stall. Every time Mum said "when are you going to move in?" I would say something like, "I haven't got enough bedding" (or cups, or plates – anything as long as I could stay where I was). Then finally at the end of October she said, "I've arranged to get your beds and things moved into the house on Sunday". Sundays at Mum's were always lovely. We had a big roast dinner and pudding and we always had a long walk over the common after, then a cup of tea and cake when we got back, and a big tea of salad, sandwiches, fresh cream cake and ice cream. Why Sunday? I said it would be better in the week, but she was having none of it. She had caught on by then that I didn't want to go, but she couldn't ask me if I wanted to stay because I would have said yes, so no more was said.

The dreaded Sunday arrived, the day I had always loved most at my parents. Now it felt strange getting out of my bed for what I saw as for the last time after all those years. I was rather dramatic about it, I was told later. That was it, my life was over. I was about to become a true single parent, all alone, miles away and two bus rides if I wanted to come back.

I still managed to spin it out until 8.30 that evening, so we had our dinner and tea, and I thought about staying for supper, but by then Mum was completely blanking me. I don't think she knew what to do next. I just wanted to throw myself at her feet and beg her not to send me away, and it felt as if she was turning her back on me. But we left, to find that our things were already there and had been all day. Dad took us and saw us in the front door, then said goodnight and left.

I was upset and angry; I had never wanted this. I thought I would stay with my mum forever. I didn't want the girls to see I was so upset, so I got their beds made up, gave them a drink and some toast and got them to bed; it took ages for them to go off, everything was so strange, but by midnight they were asleep. We had no TV or radio, very little furniture and no carpets and it was freezing in there. I had no idea how to work the central heating, so I got a bucket of water and began to wash the stairs down. The builders had left such a mess, dust everywhere and an airing cupboard full of rubble, so I just kept cleaning to keep my mind off the fact that I knew no one on this vast estate, I had no phone and didn't know where the nearest phone box was, so I couldn't get hold of Mum and Dad if something happened. I wished the ground would swallow me up. I kept going till 3 am before I had to give in, make up my bed and try to sleep, waiting for the light.

I managed to work the central heating the next day after studying the leaflet on the inside of the cupboard for about four hours: "How to light your new boiler in three easy steps". I did it without calling my Dad, which sometimes had its drawbacks. Although he was an engineer, he had very little patience with things like that and he could have blown us all to kingdom come.

I got the girls into the local school. Louise adjusted very well, Jane didn't. She had always been shy at school and struggled to make new friends. However, after a few months at the new school she began to open up and started to make friends. She was changing into a girl I hardly knew, but she seemed happy enough. I think it was the freedom she was experiencing after all the years of being rather sheltered by my parents, and she was revelling in it. I enjoyed seeing her with this new confidence she had never had before.

That week after moving in we caught the bus three times to visit my grandmother's shop about twelve miles away to see her. Mum was hoping she would ask us back for some tea, but she didn't. I think she was getting fed up with us turning up and just sitting there, and I guess she must have been worried that I might not be coping on my own with the girls. She must have had to be strong to keep turning me away, and much as I took that to heart I know now that she did the right thing for me. I had to grow up at last.

It wasn't just looking after the girls alone, as I had done that every day since they were born – it was everything else, like budgeting to pay bills (I had never paid a bill in my life), buying enough food for the week without spending all my allowance, and then there was the RENT MAN. Dear God, he frightened the life out of me. Every Monday, I think it was, he came to collect the rent from me. I can't remember how much it was, maybe £5 a week, and I had to make sure I had this cash on me. We used to have to wait for him to come and we couldn't go out until then. I used to hover near the front door ready to open it the moment he knocked so that I didn't miss him, although I don't know why. I used to jump out of my skin because he didn't knock normally, he used to bang and thump so loud, usually about eight times, and I was too scared to open the door until this onslaught stopped. Then, trembling, I slowly opened the front door. He was huge and very serious and ugly, with a voice to match his knock. He would bellow the amount he wanted, grab it off me, scribble in my rent book, throw the book back at me and go. No "goodbye" or "see you next week". Maybe he had to be that way in his line off work, with his "pay me now or die" kind of look. But I think he was a natural at it. Soon after I moved in they stopped the door-to-door rent collections and we had to pay it ourselves, which was such a relief for me.

Hard as I tried I was always broke by Saturday. The girls had dancing lessons every Saturday morning and the last of my money went on them. Sometimes I had enough to catch the bus into town and sometimes we walked the three miles, either way we always ended up at my grandmother's shop at about 1pm, and we either got the bus or walked there as well. Mum was getting used to this, so she had lunch ready for us when we got there, and then we went into town together for shopping. Then, because I had told her my money wouldn't stretch for the weekend food, we began to go back with my parents every weekend. So I had my weekends back at Mum and Dad's. I loved it and so did the girls, and I know Mum and Dad did too. Sunday evening Dad used to take us back home and I didn't mind then, I knew I had next weekend to look forward to.

It didn't take me too long to make a couple of friends, through the friends the girls made. One woman in particular became a very good friend; she was a single parent too, with two kids. After that I didn't feel so alone. My neighbours were all lovely and all young like me, and I began to actually like being there. I began to see the house as my home at last, but we still stayed at Mum and Dad's every weekend.

The money was always tight and juggling it every week was a nightmare. I never asked my parents for anything if I could help it, and I knew they were still having problems with my brother. The girls were now mixing with a different breed of child, fashion-conscious kids. I didn't have the money to make the clothes they wanted, especially Jane, who was coming up eleven years old, so I used to trawl around the charity shops for clothes and material that I could unpick, wash and iron to make some clothes for them. They never knew where the material came from or they would never have worn them. I was very good at sewing, so apart from buying the odd pattern now and then it didn't cost me anything and they looked really good. Some of the other women on the estate who saw Jane's latest clothes asked if I could make the same for their daughters. I turned them down as I didn't really have the time, but I did do alterations for them and that was a handy bit of pocket money.

My brother would come around once a week to see me, I don't know why. He would have a cup of tea, read his newspaper and then leave. Maybe I would get 'hello' and 'bye' but not much else – he didn't want to talk to me or anyone. I was finding him really strange, but I thought it was just something he was going through.

A few months later Mum told me that James and Stella were splitting up. I knew he had been spending quite a bit of time at Mum's lately; he was there most weekends when I went. He was always lying on the bed reading, completely alone and isolated within himself, I thought. I began to worry about him. James and Stella did get back together again, but it was to be for the last time.

I started to work with my Mum and Nan in the shop three days a week and that really helped. It wasn't much, but it used to pay my bus fare there and back, and I used to be given a bag of fruit and veg which was well past its sell-by date, but if I got home quickly enough they could be used for the girls' tea. My Nan was careful with money to put it politely, so tight that when she held her hand out to give me a pound for cleaning her flat I used to have to grab the coin and pull to get her to let go of it. Mum used to slip me a couple of quid now and then without Nan knowing as there would have been uproar. My Nan had quite a temper, and my mum never learnt how to stand up to her. It was Nan's East End upbringing. She was the youngest of twelve children, with a Jewish father who had been disowned by his family for marrying out of his faith, and from the stories she told me they lived in absolute poverty, sharing her brother's shoes so that they could take turns in going to school, walking over Waterloo Bridge at first light to beg barrow boys for scraps of anything they could eat. My head is full of the tales she told me, and I understand why she was like that – she was tough, she'd had to be or she wouldn't have survived. That was always in her; she didn't know how to be any other way. So I was a little scared of her, but I had great respect for what she had achieved in her 89 years.

The car Mum had bought a few months before was standing around at her place going rusty from lack of use. She was getting the hang of driving pretty well, but she was so nervous on the road and in the end it got the better of her and she stopped having lessons. I think she thought she would try again, but she never did. She decided I could use it, but she made it very clear that it was still her car and that if my brother wanted to use it he could. That was OK.

God, what a difference it made, after all those years of walking everywhere and waiting for buses. I could drop the girls off at school and be at the shop in ten minutes. I didn't have to carry bags of shopping everywhere now, I could get them to their dancing lessons on time and we didn't have to be up at the crack of dawn. I loved the car and it cost about the same in petrol as the bus fares. My brother didn't use it much, but when he did take it he would be gone for days with it and that used to annoy the hell out of me. Mum couldn't see the problem; I guess I had begun to rely on it. It didn't make for good feelings between my brother and me, and I started to resent him. It always seemed to me he could get away with blue murder. If I had taken the car for a few days there would be no end to the questions I would have been asked. It was like that for the next few months, and then the car broke down and neither of us could use it until it was fixed. I did make a point of saying to my Mum that it was most likely the way he had driven it that had caused the problem.

CHAPTER 8

A tragedy

~ele~

During that summer of 1977 I met a man. I had been down town with Mum and she told me she had seen some really nice duvets that she wanted to buy for the girls' beds. They were in one of the shops Mum often went into to buy things – she knew the woman who worked there and she said how nice she was. It was a kitchen-cum-allsorts kind of a shop on two floors. We went upstairs to look at the duvets and bought two.

The woman was tying them up for me so they wouldn't be too bulky to carry on the bus when a very large man came through a door into the shop. He came straight over to us and started to chat. He was a very friendly guy, and I assumed it was the woman's husband. He offered to deliver them to me that evening about 7.30 to save carrying them, so I said, "Yes great, thanks". At 7.30 sharp he knocked at my door and handed the duvets to me, then said "Hello again, any chance of a cup of tea?"

I was a bit taken back. He looked quite a bit older than me and I assumed he was married, so with that I just said "no" and "goodbye" and that was that. I remember thinking I wouldn't go back to that shop again, and wondering what Mum would say when I told her.

The next morning there was a knock at my door and there he was again, standing there just smiling at me. After what seemed like an age he said "I asked my partner in the shop what I should do. I find you really pretty and nice, and she said 'There's no harm in asking', so here I am."

"Oh your partner, I thought she was your wife," I said. He fell about laughing and said, "No no, she's the reason I'm here, it's her wedding anniversary next week and I wondered if you would like to come to the party with me, seeing as she knows your mum. She said you can go into the shop to check it out if you want."

I needed time to think, so I said I would phone the shop tomorrow and let John know (that was his name).

As soon as he left I phoned Mum and told her what had just happened, and for the first time, without me having to work on her, she said "You go, I'll look after the girls for you". I nearly passed out in the phone box.

I phoned the shop the next day and told John "Yep OK, I'll go with you". "Great" he said and gave the phone to his partner, who laughed and said she couldn't believe that I thought they were married. She said she would love to see me there, so it was done, and so began the next fourteen years of my life.

I had a great time with John, and he was so outgoing, so different from me. People began to notice a change in me; he made me laugh and he brought me out of myself a little more. Once or twice a week he took me out, and Mum never complained – I think she thought she would see me settled at last. He took me to places I hadn't been before, mixing with adults, wining and dining, and I loved every minute of it.

Then suddenly, after about six months I wasn't seeing him as often. He said he thought we should leave it for a while, that he wasn't ready to become too involved at the moment. Of course my pride was dented and I was upset, but we parted on good terms and I didn't see him again for about a year.

Meanwhile life carried on as normal. Mum's car had been fixed and James and I were sharing it again, but he wasn't so bothered about it this time so I got to use it more. I was still staying at Mum's every weekend, working for my Nan through the week. I noticed that my brother was spending more and more time at Mum's through the week and weekends, just lying on the bed all day reading. He had always loved music, but now you never heard him play any more and I think he sold his guitar. He didn't seem to have any interest in anything or anyone. I was finding it hard to believe my dad was putting up with this kind of behaviour from him knowing how Dad could be. It wasn't until much later that I found out why he had tolerated it. James and his wife finally split for good, and he came back to live with our parents.

It must have been September 1977 when my parents came to tell me my brother had been in a car crash. He had gone through the windscreen of the car he was driving – a car he had stolen. He had hit a lamp post, been thrown out and landed several feet in front of the car. He had a friend in the passenger seat and he was OK. I never knew who this friend was, but he had said that just before James had hit the lamp post he had put his arm across his friend's chest as if to protect him. I don't know how true this, only what was said in the hospital.

My brother had major swellings to his face, head and chest and stitches all over his face, but he survived. When he left hospital later he was taken

straight to the police station for questioning then
released on bail.

When he was out, he told my parents he wanted to
see me. I hadn't seen him since before the crash, so the
shock of it was awful. I didn't recognise him. What a
mess he was in, and yet as I cuddled him I could sense
a kind of calm in him and it seemed like my brother
was back again. He told me not to worry and we went
into the sitting room and all had a cup of tea and
carried on as if nothing had happened. This was how
my parents dealt with things; they didn't. But they
were becoming very concerned for my poor brother.

On Wednesday October 12 1977, like any other
day, I went to Nan's shop to work. It was a beautiful
warm sunny day. Mum was already there. She looked
worried, and told me that James had to go to court that
morning because of the driving offence in September.
That was the first I had heard about the court hearing,
as they had told me nothing. I had seen James on
Sunday and he hadn't mentioned it to me. He was
lying on the bed reading when I stuck my head in the
room to say goodbye, and he didn't seem bothered
about anything. Mum said she had woken him up just
before she left for work this morning. She had ironed
his shirt and trousers to wear to court and left him two
pounds for his fare into town. He had promised to
phone at about noon to let her know the outcome in

court. It was half day in the shop on Wednesday and we closed at 1pm. We still hadn't heard anything from him, so Mum went home one way and I went the other.

At about 7 pm that night there was a knock on the door. It was my parents' next-door neighbour, and she looked terribly upset. She said she had some bad news and told me to sit down, so I sat down on the stairs. I thought "It's my dad something's happened to him".

Then she told me James was dead. She lit me a cigarette and I can't remember much after that, but I know I didn't cry. When I think back about how I felt I don't think I felt anything; I was numb with shock. I lost track of time and forgot the girls were in the sitting room watching TV. Then I remember Mum's neighbour opening my front door, and in came Mum. She looked straight at me and said "Phone your cousins", then walked straight into the sitting room with the girls.

My dad came in next, and I've never seen such grief on someone's face in all my life. He went into the kitchen and just leaned against the sink, crying. Mum's neighbour's husband had brought them to me as Dad couldn't have driven. I went into the sitting room and told the girls to go to bed as Uncle James had had an accident and Nan and Gramp would be staying with us that night. I sometimes think they knew how bad it was, because normally they would have wanted to stay up with Nan and Gramp there, but they made no fuss, just went to bed for me like good girls.

I went and phoned my cousins. Mum always went to them before she asked me to do anything, so I thought nothing of it. After that I went to my friend's house, as I couldn't bear to go back home to that terrible silence. She made me some tea and she cried but I still couldn't. I stayed for as long as I could and then had to go back. The neighbours had waited for me to get back and then they went home.

Mum never looked at me, and I don't think she had cried. I went to my dad and he put his arms around me and said "look after your mother", and we cried.

There was a knock at the door again, this time the cousins. As soon as Mum saw them she changed. She began to talk and cry while I sat on the floor and watched, wondering why she wouldn't look at me. He was my brother, he was dead, and I needed someone to hold on to me. Then as she sat talking she said, "He was always my favourite" and put her head on my cousin's shoulder and cried. I didn't know what to do. I felt so sorry for my Mum, but for just a moment my love for her became mixed up with hate. I had to let it go, this wasn't the time. I look back to that night, which is etched into my soul, and see a small young girl overwhelmed with grief sitting in a corner on the floor with her arms wrapped around herself, and no one taking any notice of her, apart from telling her to put the kettle on.

Later that night Stella came round, and she was distraught. Mum took her upstairs to my bedroom and they were both crying. I heard my sister-in-law say she had always loved him and my Mum said "Yes I know you did". But so did I, Mum!

I got into bed with Louise that night while Mum and Dad had mine. Then the tears came silently streaming down my face, and I said goodbye to my brother alone.

I didn't send the girls to school for the next couple of days; everything was crazy. Mum would still not talk to anyone, nor would Dad. The atmosphere was dreadful; they wouldn't even look at each other. I wanted to get a doctor in for them, but they were having none of it. I was completely lost, I just didn't know what to do, and it was like walking on eggshells. The TV was switched off, I couldn't play my music, and it was complete misery. I know we all deal with death differently, but I just wanted to cry and let Mum see that I needed some comfort. I couldn't be like them, completely detached from their feelings. I didn't see my Mum or Dad cry again until the funeral.

The next day we had to go and break the news to my Nan, so I left the girls with a neighbour. I didn't know how Nan was going to react; she had not long ago lost her own daughter and son, both in their early forties. I did know that she didn't deal with her feelings either, but I thought maybe for me she might be different. As I went in to the shop, she had already been told what had happened, and she was standing in the shop, arms folded across her chest, looking completely blank. I went up to her hoping for a cuddle, but she threw her hands up in front of her face and told me to go away. She might as well have slapped me around the face. I should have known better.

The funeral was arranged for the following week, a church service and then on to the crematorium. As we were following the coffin into the church it began to rain very lightly. Mum said "God is crying for him" and she took my arm briefly, the first time she had ,ouched me since James had died, and the last. After the cremation we all gathered outside and again I was completely alone. I just leaned up against a wall and cried.

My dad had found my brother. He was going to put his car into the garage and as he lifted the door up he saw a car inside with its lights on. He looked and saw my brother inside and thought he was asleep, but when he touched him he knew he was dead. Mum told me much later that Dad had just fallen through the kitchen door, screaming "He's dead, he's dead!" My poor poor dad. The neighbours heard the screams and went round to see what was wrong, and when they saw they called the police and ambulance.

James had left two short notes in the car, one for my parents to say he was sorry and one for Stella saying, "Don't let the children forget me".

My parents stayed with me for the next six months. My mum never went back to that house again; they rented it out while they waited to sell it. As time went by it all began to make sense to me. Mum told me that the night before James had died she had been sitting watching TV waiting for him to come home. It was midnight when she noticed car headlights in the field at the back of our garden. Mum just thought it was someone parking in the village hall car park. Five minutes later James came in and went straight to bed; she didn't see him to talk to. In the morning, after she had woke him up, he got up and went into the bathroom; she still hadn't spoken to him. She went into his bedroom to make his bed, as she always did. She noticed small pieces of glass and some blood on the sheets. Mum being Mum, she chose to ignore it and called out "Bye, don't forget to phone me later".

We knew then that the car she had seen was the car he had stolen. He had smashed the window, and that's where the glass and blood had come from. He had waited for Mum to go to work, then driven the car into the garage and ended his life with a hosepipe he had rigged up to the exhaust.

When Mum got home that Wednesday, she found his shirt and trousers and the two pounds where she had left it for him. She guessed he hadn't gone to court, but she couldn't understand why the money was still there; James always needed money, it didn't make sense. Mum just carried on with her day. One thing she did every Wednesday was to sweep the drive, so she went to open the garage door to get the broom out, but it had been placed outside the garage. She found that strange, but thought no more of it. My brother meant to kill himself, and even in the terrible state his mind must have been in he had a lucid moment and thought about Mum and put the broom outside.

I learnt later that James had made four other suicide attempts and had been hospitalized each time, and on each occasion he had discharged himself. They wanted my parents to sign him into psychotherapy, but think the stigma attached to that would have been too much for them to bear, so it was ignored. I think they thought it was just something he was going through. That was why there was no pressure from my dad towards James. That was why he had let him get away with so much. Everything was making sense now. If only they could have shared this with me, I might have been able to help, but I'll never know.

It had to happen after Mum and Dad moved in with me – Mum and I fell out. I didn't mind the fact that they had my bed, but I was sharing a single bed with one of the girls, usually Louise because she was the smallest, and they never asked how we were managing. Nine times out of ten I used to throw a blanket on the floor and sleep there. I didn't complain as they had enough to deal with, but after three months they didn't seem to be going anywhere. They never mentioned moving, and I began to get a bit frustrated. I thought they could at least have offered to get another bed for me to sleep in.

Anyway, the only mirror in the house was in my bedroom and one day I was in there getting changed to take the girls out. I tried to only ever go in there when Mum was busy or at work, but this evening she was home. She knew I was in there as I had some music on, and without knocking she walked straight in. I think I tutted or something like that, and that was it, World War Three erupted in my bedroom.

Mum and Dad had helped me quite a lot while they stayed with me. They gave me the carpet from their house and bought me a really lovely black and white unit for my books and glasses. I didn't have to buy food; I had no worries while they stayed. I hate to say this, but when Mum gave me anything she would always use that in an argument, so I got "After all we've done for you, etc etc." She wiped the floor with me.

Within three months they had moved out, but she had made me feel so guilty. I never spent another weekend with them. It was the girls and me again. I had at last learnt to stand on my own two feet, and the feeling was good. My parents were starting to pick up the pieces of their lives and begin again, but it was never the same. I didn't notice any real change in them. They were good at being normal but I knew they were not OK.

I still helped out at my Nan's shop a few times a week, and Nan began to get more and more confused as time went on, so they decided to sell up and get her into a warden-controlled bungalow. Nan became so muddled in her thinking that she was a problem to the wardens. Mum kept getting phone calls. Nan would leave the kettle on and forget it, she started lighting candles at night to save on electricity, and she would wander off down the road looking for a bus stop, the bus that would take her home to her mum. In the end she was such a danger to herself and everyone else there that Mum bought her a home to live with her and Dad, who wasn't over the moon as they had never got on.

One morning I was walking the girls to school when an almighty JCB pulled up alongside me. I didn't take much notice, just a man at work I thought, until I heard "Hello sweetheart, how are you?"

It was John. I didn't know what to say. The traffic was piling up behind this great big machine and I felt all the other mums looking, and felt a right idiot. We had a quick chat because of all the traffic, tooting, swearing and so on from some of the motorists, and I was going redder by the minute. We met later that week for a meal, and began where we had left off a year ago.

This time there would be no break for a few years. John and I started to see each other on a regular basis. He made me happy and he made me laugh, something I had never done much before. The girls liked him and Mum and Dad did too, although maybe Mum more than Dad. I think she was secretly hoping that I would at last settle down. We had two years together, and then one day out of the blue he said, "I suppose we should do something about making this more permanent between us". That was John's proposal. He didn't have a romantic bone in his body but he had a lot of other qualities, which were hard to find in most men.

Mum was over the moon. She got so overcome she couldn't get her breath, and I thought she was going to be a stretcher case. I had never seen such an emotional outpouring from her before. Dad's words were "You could do a lot worse". I didn't know quite what to make of that, but I guess he was happy for me. Mum took over. She organized a huge engagement party, bought me a really lovely lace dress and invited everyone she knew –I just let her get on with it. I suppose after the grim affair with Dick, she wanted to show me off as a proper bride-to-be.

Not long after that a house a couple of doors up from John's mum came on the market. We went to look at it, made an offer and with a little financial help from my dad for the deposit we bought it. It needed gutting as it hadn't been touched since 1926 when it had been built, no hot water and just one cold water pipe in the kitchen. It was a challenge, but we were young and we gave ourselves a year to do it up. We worked every weekend and most evenings on the house and the girls got involved too. It was exciting for all of us to have our first home together. We finished almost a year to the day later and a week before our wedding.

Meanwhile back to Mum's world and the wedding she was busy planning. I didn't want a big fluffy dress and she accepted that. I thought she would try and get me into one, but she was fine about it. I think it was that close to my wedding day she did not dare upset me in case I called it off. I was dreading the day. I was still quite shy and the thought of all those people – four hundred to be exact. I don't know how it came to that, in fact I don't remember sending any invitations out –

Mum again of course.

When the day dawned I had to go and pinch some of my dad's booze which he hid in the airing cupboard – he didn't know I knew where it was. I didn't get drunk but I got a bit tipsy just to get myself through the day. That was when I realized there was something to this alcohol business. My girls were bridesmaids and they looked lovely.

The day went well, but I was troubled; I didn't know why. Too late now, I thought. A close friend of mine offered to take the girls back with her for the night so John and I could have our first night together alone. She need not have bothered; we went home to our new home and within five minutes John was snoring. As I said, not a romantic bone in his body, bless him.

We had a good first four years, during which time we adopted Emmy my Old English Sheep dog, and I loved her she really was my dog. I was pregnant with my third child in 83 and had a pretty rough time of it having high blood pressure and preeclampsia again and a four week stay in hospital before they induced me. There she was, my Lucy, all 7lbs 15oz of her, with lots of hair like her sisters and beautiful just like them. Louise had passed her twelve plus and was doing really well bless her, and Jane had signed herself into care. Here we go again...

We had been having problems with Jane for the last year. At first everything was fine at home, then almost overnight she changed into a girl I didn't know, it really was that sudden. She had been going to the same school for the last year and I wasn't aware of her having any problems until I got a call from the school asking why she hadn't been to school for the last few weeks. I told them I had taken her every day. They assured me that she hadn't been, so then we both knew she had been truanting. I couldn't believe this had been going on for about three weeks without me knowing.

I waited for her to come home on the bus and asked her about it. She denied it until I said I had had a call from the school. She said she didn't want to go to the school any more as she didn't like the kids there.

I spoke to the Head at school the next day and decided to get her into a local school a bit closer to home. She started there just two weeks later, and we thought that she would be fine. But over the next two years, things got steadily worse. She began stealing from everyone, family and friends, constant lying, skipping school, disappearing in the middle of the night and going missing for two days at a time. At the age of fourteen that was an awful worry. I began to have dizzy spells and felt unwell with the strain of it all, so the doctor put me on tranquillisers just to help me get through the day at work. I tried everything from trying to talk to her to stopping treats, to crying and begging her to stop behaving the way she was, but after two years of this I really began to give up she had worn me out. We were quite often woken up at three in the morning by police wanting to search the house, her bedroom and her.

Then one day we got a call from the police to say that Jane had gone to the police station and told them she didn't want to go home. She was asking for my dad to pick her up and take her home, which he did. Social Services got involved. They spoke to Jane and it turned out that the last two years had all been about John. She said she hated him and didn't want to go home with him there. They told me she seemed extremely jealous of our relationship, something I hadn't been aware of. This really shook me up, because John was such a kind man and so good with the girls.

Jane wouldn't come home and she didn't want to stay with her grandparents, so she signed herself into care, and from that moment I lost all rights as a parent. It almost destroyed me.

I took her to the place that would be her home for the next two years and they showed us upstairs to her room, just Jane and me. I looked at her and my heart was breaking. I asked her if this was what she really wanted, and she just looked back at me like a little girl lost with tears in her eyes. I knew she didn't want to stay, but she had signed those bloody forms and they would not let her go. I just wanted to grab her and run away from it all, but instead I was asked to say goodbye. I took another long look at her told her I loved her and that I would phone when I got home. Then I walked out of that room and left her standing there all alone and so frightened and I couldn't do a thing about it. I cried all the way home.

Jane was gone from me for almost two years, and apart from the odd weekend when we were allowed to go and see her I never heard how she was doing. We were even denied phone calls to her. When she got really ill once, no one told me. They take all your rights as a parent away.

But life went on while Jane was away. I had Louise to think about and she was doing really well at school, but it had affected all of us and although she didn't say much about Jane I knew she must have been struggling like the rest of us while all that was going on. I feel now I neglected Louise by not asking her how she felt about it all and if it was affecting her studying. I just assumed she was coping, and bless her, she never complained. Jane just consumed my every waking hour – I couldn't think about anything else.

John and I were still busy working on the house and garden while Jane was busy getting into more trouble.

The two years away had done her no good whatsoever in fact after mixing with all kinds in there at sixteen she came home very streetwise. Again I had no idea where she was or who she was with. In the end after a few months she moved out and went to live with her grandparents and managed to hold down a job for the next two years, so we all had some peace at last.

Louise was still at school and doing well despite all the upheaval her sister had caused. It's a good job I only had one like that or I would have signed myself away years ago!

All was peaceful on the home front, but I knew it wouldn't last. Lucy became very unwell when she was just seventeen months old, and for a month we were back and forth to the doctor's. She was losing weight quickly, couldn't keep anything down, even water, and she screamed every now and then and rolled around the floor in pain. I was out of my mind with worry. The doctors kept saying it was gastric and sending us home. Then, after I had called the doctor every day for two weeks, they decided to take her into hospital. They said she was constipated, so they gave her a pessary to clear the blockage – she screamed, I cried. The doctor said if she was no better in the morning they would have to insert a drip. Thank God she was better, so we went home, but that night we rushed her back into hospital as she was vomiting and screaming with pain. They called for another doctor from another hospital and he was there within an hour. While my little girl lay in my arms exhausted from the pain, no food, not much in fluids in the last month, at last they were going to do something for her. I began to pray again that whatever was wrong with her I would have the strength to cope with it for her sake. I thought I was going to lose her; she only weighed seventeen pounds, a pound for every month she had been alive.

The doctor was lovely. He calmed me down and said he was going to help. He sat for a long time listening to her tummy with his stethoscope and then ordered X-rays. The X-rays had to be done twice – John and I had to stand her up while I held her arms stretched up in the air and John had to hold her legs apart while she screamed in pain. I still have dreams about this and when they put the drip in her little foot they had to hold her down to do that. I couldn't stand to hear her screams any more so I ran out of the room and kept running until I couldn't hear her.

She was taken down for an op. The doctor told me that there was a blockage but he wasn't sure why; he also said he might have to remove some of the bowel. Those three hours were the longest of my life. A nurse came to fetch us and said the surgeon wanted to see us. I thought I was going to pass out walking down to theatre. John told me to take deep breaths and as the nurse pushed open the theatre doors in the distance I saw the surgeon smiling. Thank God, I thought. He told us that when he had opened her up her ovary had popped out. It had twisted and gone black and was three times its normal size, which was what had caused the blockage. He had removed it, along with her fallopian tube, and had taken her appendix out too. He also said, "Another week and we could have lost her". I can still see this doctor's smiling face. I can't remember his full name –I think he was Greek – but they called him Dr Mac. I know he saved my daughter's life and I will never forget him.

Now all we had to do was get my little Lucy well again, and within a week she was rushing around everywhere again, thanks to God and Dr Mac.

Jane said she wanted to help me while I was nursing Lucy back to health at home, and I was grateful to her for this. John had to work and Mum as well, and Lucy was still sore from the operation so I didn't want to strap her into a car seat, which made going shopping difficult. So Jane said she would do the shopping etc for me. She was a big help and I thought we had turned a corner. As the year went on Lucy was back to good health, and things were at last on an even keel.

CHAPTER 9

Devon

Mum and Dad had been thinking of moving to Devon for some time and had been to look at some properties there. John and I also wanted to move there, but for us it wasn't the right time. They found an old thatched cottage which they fell in love with and moved within a few months, and God I missed them. It felt odd to have them so far away, so I decided with John to move as soon as possible and have a fresh start for all of us.

I had a miscarriage in 1984. I didn't want Lucy to be an only child because of the age gap between my older girls and her, and she would have been alone growing up without her siblings.

In 1985 my left arm went completely numb. I could use it and move it, but it was just numb. I went to the doctors and he said it was most likely the side effects of a migraine, although I hadn't had a headache, so I went home. John's mum had been looking after Lucy while I had been to the doctors and I went in to hers and put the kettle on to make a cup of tea for us both. While we were sitting drinking the tea, I suddenly realised that I couldn't feel the left side of my body, from my shoulder down to my ankle. I told her and she looked so worried – I think she thought, like me, that I was having a stroke. She told me to go straight back to the doctor's, though thinking about it now an ambulance should have been called.

Anyway I got back to the doctor's and he saw me straight away. I had pins stuck in me back and front of my body, but I couldn't feel them. Then another doctor came in to examine me. Then they both disappeared. As they went out of the room I could see patients waiting on the landing to be seen. The waiting room was full up, I had been in that room being prodded and poked for over an hour and the patients had been building up. I kept thinking "please God don't let them send for an ambulance and carry me out on a stretcher in front of all these people".

The two doctors came back into the room looking worried. They said I would need to be admitted to hospital and they would be expecting me early that same evening. Then they let me go. Outside so many people were staring at me and some looked angry while some looked concerned. I got out of there as soon as I could and went back to my mother-in-law's and told her they wanted me to go into hospital and run a few tests. I told her I would let her know tomorrow how I got on. She looked terribly worried.

I got home and told John what had happened, and as usual he didn't seem particularly interested, just concerned about how he would cope with Lucy. I told him he would have to take time off work till this was sorted. It was John's way of coping with anything stressful in life – he would just bury his head in the sand.

They admitted me and kept trying to give me tablets for my headache, but I kept telling them I didn't have a bloody headache. I was in the hospital for twelve days. My mum and dad knew I was there, but they never called once to talk to me or see how I was, so on the fifth day I called them. It was awkward. Mum didn't really want to talk as she didn't cope with real life. She just said that they wouldn't be up to see me as they had to look after my Nan. I did love my Nan, but I did resent her too sometimes as Mum always put her first, even with this. I would have loved my mum and dad to come and see me and tell me I would be OK, but as ever the conversation was cut short and I didn't hear from them for weeks, not even to see if I had come out of hospital and what had been wrong. I just thought, fuck 'em.

As the days went on the numbness went, and by the time I was discharged it had completely gone. They did loads of tests and X-rays and finally decided that I had been in contact with someone who had mumps, which I had, my brother when we were small, but I had never caught them. They said they thought I had contracted them but instead of getting them I had just carried the virus and it had hatched out in my central nervous system and caused me to go numb.

I had to go back and see the consultant after three months and he said I should be OK now and asked me how I felt. I said I was fine, except that the little finger on my left hand would go into spasm now and then.

My Catherine was born in 1986, another beautiful daughter. I still remember when she was born how her eyes were wide open, looking everywhere, no crying, just looking, as if to say "Ah, this could be fun". And as she grew she was a live wire, full of energy, and still is.

Nine weeks after Catherine was born Jane presented me with my first granddaughter. In 1987, Louise gave me my first grandson. Jane gave me my second grandson the same year, and Louise gave me another granddaughter in 1989. My little family was growing fast.

We moved to Devon in 1986, so we had a really nice place for the girls and ourselves and John's mum. It didn't take long for Jane to join us with her husband and two little ones. They rented a cottage a couple of miles from us and we saw each other every day. It was good for the children to grow together and there was always plenty of noise and laughter.

Louise and her husband made a few visits. It all seemed idyllic, beautiful house and all my family around me just the way I liked it, and then Mike happened.

Mike, Jane's husband, was a friendly kind of guy and good with kids. At the same time he was a player, someone who liked to make a quick buck off someone else's back. John and Mike became friends, and soon they began to talk about selling the place we had just bought and running some kind of business between them, which seemed kind of odd because we were the only ones with money. Anyway Mike was a real smooth talker and we were sucked in by the idea of getting rich quick. We were still quite young and we thought we would at least go and look at some places. Within five months we had moved miles away into a transport café-cum-restaurant. No one had twisted my arm, but I knew this was going to be one of the biggest regrets of my life.

It was agreed that Mike would not be a partner in the business, which seemed to upset him. We said he could work for us and take a wage, and live rent free in the mobile home we had bought, if he would do the PR work and attract business; we also said he could eat in the café free when he wanted. It didn't seem enough; things went from good to bad to worse. Some nights we would watch him take a full optic bottle of drink from the restaurant back to his mobile home. His PR work consisted of inviting total strangers in and giving them free drink and leaving one hell of a mess in the bar for us to clean up the next morning.

I think that was one of the busiest and loneliest times in my life, trying to look after my mother-in-law and two small girls. I loved it and hated it. We were in the middle of nowhere, really beautiful country and fantastic views, an acre of ground around the bungalow we lived in that adjoined the café and restaurant, and a swimming pool that had seen better days, but we were hoping to get that sorted as time went on.

Within two months or so, Louise and her husband Andrew, plus my first grandson, who was about 18 months old, moved into a mobile home we had bought for them to live in. It was next to Jane's, in the grounds of our property. It all sounded perfect to me to have all my girls together. Of course, it didn't last.

My son-in-law was going to Exeter University, which wasn't around the corner from us, so I was letting him learn to drive in my car and every morning and afternoon he did the driving to the railway station. That was fine, but I think it all got too much for both of them in the end. They were young, and with a small baby, I guess they felt trapped and I think they missed the other very big part of their life, the Salvation Army. They didn't stay too long, a few months or so and then they left to go home and live with Andrew's parents. I felt awful, and blamed myself for them wanting to leave, though I know now I wasn't that. They just needed a bit of life around them, not lots of fields and nothing else.

So that was that. I missed them terribly, and was beginning to become really depressed. It was a combination of looking after my mother-in-law, much as I loved her, the girls, the café when I could, the draughty old wooden bungalow with no heating in it that five of us lived in, a crumbling old pool outside that was a constant worry when the little ones went outside to play, and Mike.

Mike was a law unto himself. As I said before, he wanted partnership without contributing a single penny to the business, which we had bought. We would see him going back to the mobile home with a large bottle of vodka under his arm, and this was happening almost every night. Mike and Jane used to go off most days and leave a mess behind that he had created the previous night while entertaining.

John and I had had enough. Late one night while we were sitting adding up the day's takings in the kitchen Mike came in. He had had a bit to drink and I can't remember exactly how it started, but I remember saying that I had had enough of him and what a sod he was. He came towards me in a threatening way and it really frightened me. John's reaction was so quick – he had his hands around the neck and basically lifted him off the floor and put him outside. We were both shaken up. Mike just slunk off back to the mobile.

The next morning I watched Mike walking between the mobile and the café and I could see the marks of John's fingers around his neck. I thought, that was a long time coming, bloody good job.

He began getting the car that we had bought them ready to tow away the mobile home that we had also bought them– when I say them, I really mean Mike. John and I had agreed to let him take the lot and go. Jane wanted to go with him and I needed to know that she and the children would have somewhere to live and something to sell if they needed a deposit on a flat or something.

So that was that – they were gone.

I was so unhappy that the perfect little world I had created in my mind had failed. Now I also had a marriage that was heading for disaster. We hadn't been talking since the time we had bought the café. I had been unsure about it, and I was right. I kept trying to keep optimistic and pushed down the feelings of dread that kept me awake most nights. I knew there was only one way for this to go, and it wasn't going to be good.

We got a goat for the garden to help keep the grass down – we called her Polly. I loved that goat, and so did Lucy and Catherine. She was a little bit of pleasure, along with Emmy the dog. I'm not sure if it was living in a café or just being an animal lover, but I had also gradually become the keeper of ten cats, most of them feral and one very young pregnant one, plus my own beautiful ginger tom, Selwyn. I loved looking after them. One very old cat I brought inside and took care of because she had constant sinus problems and couldn't breathe properly, so I had to clean her nose before she could eat or drink. I did run up a few vet bills but I wouldn't let them suffer. The little feral pregnant cat, Scatty we called her, had four kittens, but she was just a kitten herself and didn't really know how to look after them, so I used to go into the large barn where she and the others lived and have a little look to see how she was getting on. One day when I went to check on her, she was gone. We found her in the snow under a hedge with her kittens, three live and one dead. I had to take the kittens back into the barn and wrap them up in their blankets. Scatty, being so wild, stayed back until I had gone indoors, and I watched as she went straight into check on them.

That evening, while I was feeding all the others I noticed Scatty had gone again with her kittens. We found her near where we had found her before, all curled up with her kittens. This time two more of her kittens were dead and only one was still alive. I had no choice but to take the last kitten indoors with me. I managed to feed her and keep her warm, but Scatty would not go back to the barn; she just stayed outside crying for her baby. It broke my heart. The next morning she was still crying, but she wouldn't let me anywhere near her and she wouldn't come indoors. As a last resort I took the kitten into the barn and laid her on her blanket, and before I could get indoors Scatty had run in and was mewling and washing this little kitten of hers frantically all over. After that Scatty stayed put and the kitten grew. The girls had named her Holly. She was white with black, brown and ginger patches – she must have got the ginger from her mum.

A week later when checking the cats again, I noticed that the new kitten couldn't open her eyes, so

I took her to the vets, leaving Scatty crying again. The vet said Scatty was washing and licking her too much and she had made her eyes sore. I had to keep her away from Scatty for at least two days to let her eyes heal, which they did, but all the time Scatty was going crazy. Then I put her with her mum and it all began again, another eye infection. So although my heart was breaking for this little mother cat, there was nothing else for it, I had to keep her with me.

It was so upsetting to hear her crying endlessly for her kitten. She was trying to pluck up the courage to come indoors, but she just couldn't. She kept looking through the windows trying to see her baby, so four or five times a day I took Holly into the barn to see her mum. It melted my heart to watch the absolute delight on Scatty's face, and she was purring so loudly. But after a few minutes she would begin washing Holly's eyes again, so I had to take her away for a while.

After a week or so Scatty stopped crying for her baby, but I still took her in every day and they were both so happy to be together for a while. I never did get to touch Scatty – being born feral, I never stood a chance. For a while Polly, the goat and all my feral cats lived quite peacefully in the barn with Holly, while Emmy and Selwyn were indoors.

I had been having what they called 'women's problems'

for some years on and off and was in so much pain in the end I had to have a hysterectomy and bowel and bladder repair jobs. Mum and Dad came to stay to help John with the girls. At this time John and I were not speaking at all. We didn't argue, because we just didn't talk. I know he was as unhappy as me – it was a complete breakdown of communication. Mum and Dad must have picked up on it but didn't say anything.

I vividly remember Lucy watching the TV some months earlier, before Mike and Jane had left, and we were all sort of okay-ish with each other. One day she saw a man and woman kissing and she asked me what they were doing, as she had never seen her own mum and dad kissing. I felt guilt and sadness for her, and Mike, who was there at the time, said she might grow up to think all relationships were like that. That hit me like a ton of bricks. I don't know what I thought our life was like. I knew I was very unhappy, but now I was risking making my girls unhappy too. It wasn't a normal family with laughter or even talking between me and their dad, it was just silence, and they had begun to think that was normal.

I had my hysterectomy and other bits done on the 3rd of January 1989 in the afternoon at Barnstaple Hospital and was wheeled back into theatre at midnight that same day, as I was bleeding internally. The next day back on the ward I was really unwell and hooked up to allsorts and having a transfusion. Mum, Dad, John and the girls came to see me, but I really wasn't up for it. Then I had 12 red roses delivered from Louise in Australia, who was hoping I was all right. I don't know if Mum had phoned her, but apparently I had been very ill and everyone had been worried. It's strange – I think I had been out of it for about twenty hours, so when I did come round I felt so comfortable and sleepy. It was a lovely feeling, but the nurses wouldn't let me lie down. They kept waking me up and propping me up in bed, something to do with the amount of anaesthetic I had been give.

Then while everyone was around the bed looking at me I began to shake uncontrollably. They said my body was rejecting the blood they were giving me. My parents had to leave with John and the girls. I was OK, but I had terrible pain the next day as my bowels expelled the blood. Then I got a massive infection and was really ill again. When I looked around the ward at the other women, who were all in there for the same thing, I was so scared and thought I might be going to die. They move me into a side ward with a bad fever and started me on an antibiotic, but it took weeks to get me well.

Most of the nurses were OK, but there a few who were absolute bitches. One of these nurses told me I needed to get into a bath but I was so ill and in so much pain that I could hardly walk. I had a catheter fitted, so this nurse held my bag and was trying to pull me along. It made me scream. She just looked at me and said "You're not doing too well, are you? I'll slow down a bit so you can keep up"! On another occasion at night they didn't bother to bring us any drinks before bed and didn't check on us. They left the ward lights on all night and didn't even pull the curtains. We could hear them laughing and chatting all through the night. If I hadn't been so unwell I would have said something, but nothing was said by anyone, so they got away with it.

I got home and went straight to bed. Mum had dinner ready for me, but I couldn't eat it. The girls were so pleased to see me and wanted to jump on the bed with me, but the thought of them bouncing next to me sent me cold. It really upset me because they had always slept with me since the breakdown of my marriage.

After a few days, I felt better. John had put the business on the market. It was 1989 and the recession had begun to hit us. I don't think it would have worked anyway, and John and I were struggling to pay the mortgage. My dad had advised John to go bankrupt, but he wanted to sell it. There was so much to do. I had to re home all the cats, but of course they couldn't be re homed as they were feral. So the Cats' Protection

League came and took them and promised me they would do their best to find homes for them. I knew in reality that wouldn't be possible and it broke my heart, but at least they wouldn't be roaming wild and half-starved. We still had Emmy, Selwyn and Holly. Sadly Holly disappeared the day before we left, and despite all the searching and calling we couldn't find her. I just hope she was found by someone who would love her. Polly had to go back to the farm we had got her from and the girls were upset about that, as she was always in the garden with them.

We also had had to get my mother-in-law settled somewhere as she was quite old and not really mobile. I felt so sorry for her. She had helped with buying our first property in Devon with some of the money from the sale of her house, and now she had lost everything too. We wouldn't be able to rent a big house and she would need the ground floor. We found her a lovely care home in Weston-Super-Mare, which was where we decided to rent somewhere so we would be close to her, although it didn't make me feel any better.

Weston was a bittersweet time for me. After being so remote for almost four years, I revelled in the hustle and bustle of this seaside town. It wasn't a huge place, quite small really compared to my home town of High Wycombe. John and I were still very unhappy, but he got a job straight away – that was what he did. I had no need to work. I never did, as he always provided well for us and I never had to worry about money, although the hundreds of thousands of pounds we had lost through bad choices and a recession weighed heavy on me, as I know it did him. We weren't that young any more, so it was hard to think about starting all over again, especially when you are both no longer in love.

I didn't know where we were going with it all, but there is one thing I'm not, and that's a quitter. I got Lucy into a good school, though Catherine was still too young. Children are so resilient – they were such good girls and they mixed well with other kids. After a few weeks, it was as if we had lived in Weston for years. Most days after school I would drive down onto the beach with the girls and they would play, and usually I would have a little picnic for them. I joined a women's fitness club and a spiritual church called the Blue Cross and loved it. I went on Friday evenings, sometimes Saturday and always on Sunday. I met some amazing people there and made some good friends. I had always been spiritual, but never belonged anywhere. Now I did and I had found my niche at last.

John wasn't interested in it at all. He just came home and went to sleep. I did try and encourage him to join something himself, as he was more of a people person than me. I thought he would enjoy getting out, but all I got was a mumbled "no".

Life went on about the same for a while. Jane and Mike had also moved to Weston and that was OK for me. I had missed the children and wondered how they were. They were fine and had rented a house just down the road from us. I needed to let the bad feelings go, and it wasn't all Mike's fault; I know he didn't help the situation, but in the beginning it was John and Mike who had wanted the café, and they were friends at the start. John never got over it. He couldn't stand the sight of Mike and to this day still holds on to what he lost, but I lost the same and I rarely think about it. The way I looked at it, we all have to lose things in this life and we had lost money, but we had, and still have, a beautiful family, thank god. The depression and mood swings got worse with him. It was my girls, Weston and the people I met there that got me through the next year.

John's mum seemed all right and I think she enjoyed the company in the care home. I took the girls as much as I could and she was always pleased to see them.

John's work was beginning to slow up, so we started to think about moving back to High Wycombe, where he had work contacts. We travelled back to look for a property to buy and we found one, not a great area but a start. We told John's mum we would be going back home and she would have stay in the care home until we had got ourselves sorted out – we had every intention of having her back to live with us.

Just before we uprooted everything again, my poor old cat Selwyn contracted feline aids and had to be put to sleep. He had been part of the family since 1976 when Louise had come running in with him after finding him and another kitten from the same litter. Every time we moved he was put in the removal van in his basket, and at each new place we moved to, he just wandered around and instantly made it his home. We never had to keep him in to stop him running away. The vet described him as 'a cat with a big character', and he was. I still miss my Selwyn. I know Emmy missed him too even it was just missing him batting her on the head with his claws whenever she walked past the high stool he used to lie on.

I went and said my goodbyes to everyone I had met in Weston. I had made more friends in that short year than all the years in other places, except for Lancashire.

Jane and Mike were going back home as well to find work. Here we go again, I thought.

CHAPTER 10

Betrayal

～elle～

We had bought a three-bed semi that had previously been used as offices. It had carpet tiles on the floors in most rooms and horizontal cream blinds in every room. That was a help to start with, but it had no central heating, just an old gas fire in each room and a gas heater on the wall at the bottom of the stairs that you had to light with a match. It scared the life out of me, so we just put a portable one in the hall instead. As it was June, it wasn't too bad, but by the time September arrived the girls and I were really starting to feel cold, so I bought an electric heater to put on the landing outside the bedroom and bathroom. That helped a bit, but it was soon to get very cold, and I don't just mean the weather. We did intend to get heating in maybe the following year, but we didn't have the money at that time.

John got work straight away and the money began coming in again. We bought a second-hand oak kitchen and John fitted it. The old kitchen had had one cupboard, a sink and pantry and that was all, so it was really the first thing on a long list of things to do. The girls had nice cabin beds that we had brought with us and other bits, so they were OK. All the walls had wood chip paper and were painted white, so they were fine for now.

John and I hadn't shared a bed for about four years at that time. He slept on the sofa or fold-out bed, and even though I didn't love him as a husband I knew this had to stop – he needed his own bed. I sold my bed and bought two singles to put in the same room. I didn't feel right about it, but I couldn't stand the thought of him on the sofa, especially as he had back problems. Anyway, the beds came; John knew I was getting them, but he didn't say anything as usual. He never did sleep in his bed – he stayed downstairs.

At this point in my marriage I was terribly unhappy. I knew I couldn't go on, but I didn't know how to end it. I was so worried about the girls, who loved their dad so much and were very close to him. I had been told on several occasions that I needed to make a decision and if I didn't I would become ill. Now although I am spiritual and have seen and heard spirit, I have also mixed with enough mediums to know they are not always truthful unfortunately, and the bad ones give the good ones a bad reputation. Thing is, the people who told me this didn't know anything about me – they were total strangers –but I was told the same thing three times over two years, the last time a month after we went back to High Wycombe. Now I know how this sounds to people who don't really believe in the afterlife, but I need to tell this story because it's part of what came next between me and John.

One early evening, I think it was a Friday, I saw John across the road talking to a woman in a car. As John was very sociable with everyone except me at the time I just thought it was another friend of his and didn't make anything out of it. This car kept pulling up across the road on quite a few evenings, and John would go running out to talk to this woman. When I thought about it, she never tooted her horn, but he always seemed to know when she was there, so they must have arranged it. OK, so we were in a marriage that was going nowhere, but we were still married, so I asked him about it. He said it was his ex-wife who lived around the corner, and they were just catching up with how his older daughters were and other stuff. I didn't like it, but I left it alone. I think maybe I was hoping this was a way out – perhaps he would just go off with her and let me go, and I wouldn't have to decide.

My niece had just had a baby and she didn't have much money, so I asked her if she would like some things I still had in the loft, cot, playpen, high chair, and she said yes, so I arranged to take them over to her on the following Sunday. I told John that I would need him to come with me to help and he didn't say anything –that's how bad it was. I had never known anybody who could be so distant and miserable all the time. It was making me ill.

Anyway he actually spoke to me that week to tell me he was going down to Weston to visit his mum. He would be going on Friday morning, so he would take the day off work and stay overnight. He said he would be back home Saturday and help me with the baby bits on Sunday. I was a bit shocked, as he actually seemed happy.

Quite late on Saturday night the phone rang and it was John. He told me he would be staying over till Sunday. I was livid, but I kept quiet and said nothing. I would say all I needed to say to his face on Sunday. When I put the phone down I knew who he was with. You would think I would be happy, a way out at last, but I was so angry I didn't sleep all night I was in such a rage, because he had gone behind my back and lied.

Early that Sunday morning, the girls and me got all the baby bits into the car and set off. Of course my sister-in-law was there, and was surprised not to see John. I think I told her he wasn't well or something. We stayed for a couple of hours, but I couldn't concentrate on talking, so we left. I had so much on my mind. The girls had asked why their dad wasn't home and I told them that he had had to work; he did that often, so they were fine with that.

We were home by four, and he wasn't there. By seven the girls wanted to know when he would be home, and I just said that he was working late. It was half term, so I let the girls stay up late. It was October and freezing cold out and we only had that one old gas fire for the whole of downstairs, so I went into the freezing arctic kitchen to boil some hot water, poured it into a bowl and put it down by the gas fire, and the girls put their feet in it and drank hot chocolate – they loved doing that. They were keeping my mind off what was happening.

Finally, at eleven, he came in. The girls were still up watching a video. He said hello to them and went into the kitchen without a word to me. I followed him, looked him in the eye and asked where he had been since Friday. Now John had a nasty habit of grinning at me if he thought he had upset me, and he did it then. My temper began to flare up. I told him to take the girls to bed then kissed them goodnight and up they went with their dad. My heart was breaking, because I knew what was about to happen. He came down half an hour later and I went up to check they were asleep.

We stood in the kitchen face to face and I asked him again where he had been and he said to see his mum. I asked who had been with him and he didn't answer, he just had that grin. I reminded him how he had let me down earlier with taking the things to my niece, and he just looked at me. So I asked one more time to tell what he had been doing and still he grinned. I remember my heart was pounding inside my chest so hard it made my head thump. I wanted to kill him, but instead I said "Go upstairs, kiss the girls, get your stuff and get out".

He stopped grinning and it looked as if I had slapped his face. He was in shock and that surprised me. He had obviously never thought I would do this. I had to tell him three times more, and he was just standing there. Then I started to raise my voice, and I think that's when the penny dropped that I meant it. Then he was gone out into that freezing cold October night.

I was in some kind of shock myself. I didn't feel

great about the prospect of being alone again and my parents were not there any more, as they lived in Devon. But most of the pain I felt was for my girls, thinking what I was going to have to tell them tomorrow. I had known John for 15 years and had been married to him for ten, and part of my heart ached for him, as he had been as unhappy as me. I hoped he would be all right and didn't wish him any harm. He had been a good father and had given us all he could, but I couldn't have taken much more of living like that.

I went upstairs and sat in the girls' bedroom. They were both sound asleep. I put my head in my hands and sobbed and cried out to spirit, because I knew what lay ahead, "Please God help me now!" and as soon as I had done that there was a loud thump on the wooden table next to me. It didn't frighten me – it gave me comfort in that dark, cold night.

To this day John doesn't know why he did what he did; nobody has ever understood it, even me. The decision had been taken out of my hands and made for me. It had nothing to do with me or John. I knew spirit, god, or angels whatever you want to call them were telling me "It will all be all right now".

The next morning, after a sleepless night, I got up before the girls and called the care home John's mum was in and asked to speak to her. She said she had been surprised at seeing her ex-daughter-in-law and granddaughter with John all coming to visit her, especially since she hadn't seen her daughter-in-law for years and because they had parted on such bad terms. I could tell by her voice that she knew something was wrong between me and John, she sounded so sad. I just told her I was checking that she had had a nice visit with them. I knew she knew I was lying. After that, on the same day, I got my friend to look after the girls while I went into town to get my divorce. I wanted out of this marriage as soon as possible, and ten months later it was absolute, I was free.

I don't think John could really accept it. I won't say all I could about what happened next, but let's just say the next five years were the hardest I had ever been through, financially that is. My parents were no help to me, John had stopped working and I didn't have a job. Lucy was eight and Catherine was five. My parents did offer to help me out if I came back to Devon, saying they would rent me a cottage, but if not I would have to get on with it. My parents had money. I didn't want it, but it was so bloody hurtful to say that. They knew I had an old banger of a car and was trying hard to get the girls to a decent school and get myself a job. It seemed as if they had all turned their backs on me, including John. I don't know to this day what I did that made them all seem to resent me, but that's how I was made to feel.

I managed to get the girls into a good school, although it was a good ten miles away. I began working as a dinner lady in the local school, about five minutes' walk from my house. Then I got another job developing photos and another doing a bit of book-keeping for a really nice man with MS, and finally a couple of jobs cleaning. All the jobs I had were for one or two hours each, so I managed to do them all, and if one of the girls was unwell I could take her with me to most of them. It was hard, and we were living from day to day.

I started to take a young boy and his sister to school along with my two, and their mum gave me five pounds every Friday for doing this. She and her husband ran the local newspaper shop and she became a real friend to me over the next few years. Most mornings I would phone the shop and ask if she could put a couple of bags of crisps or sweets, or both, and bring them out to the car when I arrived to pick up her children. Most mornings there was barely enough for the girls' breakfasts, let alone a packed lunch, so by the time Friday came I usually handed back the five pounds my friend gave me to cover the cost of all the things I had had to ask her for during the week, but it worked. Apart from the school job, I was paid on a daily basis so I would go shopping for food every day, but some days money was so tight, what with bills etc; I had to make a choice between petrol to get the girls to school and me to my jobs or go with very little dinner that night, which usually meant not eating.

I had so far avoided social security, but I couldn't go on like that. The mortgage hadn't been paid for about two months and my money wouldn't cover it, so I had to get some help. After a lot of form filling and questions they started to give me a weekly amount and they were going to pay the interest on the mortgage. I was allowed to earn a little bit each week, so I kept my job in the photo shop and things got a little bit better. A close friend of mine at the time came with me to sort out maintenance for the girls, but John had said that he couldn't give much because he had had to leave work over depression. I think he was told he had to give me twenty pounds a week. Sometimes he did, sometimes he didn't. This made for even more bad feelings between us. He did take the girls out Friday after school and Sunday afternoons and he did buy their shoes and the odd bits they needed now and then. One year it was cold and the girls needed winter school coats, so I had to phone my parents and ask for fifty pounds to get them. Mum as always answered the phone and said to me she would have to ask my father, which was what I expected. Yes, he said, all right, and he sent a cheque through the post. I had hated asking, but they never asked how I was getting on and how I was managing and I had had no choice. I never asked again. I used to torture myself sometimes and get really upset about why they were being so cold towards me. As their only surviving child they should have done more. I had four daughters and would help them if they needed it without giving it another thought. It still upsets me to this day. It was as if I had to be punished for another failed marriage, just as when I had had Jane —you know, you've made your bed and so on. Still, I try to think of it as their generation's type of behaviour, and believe that underneath all that dysfunctional fucking behaviour they loved me really, as I did them.

I can honestly say that during those five years in that cold house my few friends helped me more than anyone from my family.

I decided to start going out once a week with Jane. Maybe that wasn't such a good idea but what the hell —there was no mother to tell me I couldn't and I felt I had some catching up to do.

It was difficult with the girls for a few weeks. I just kept telling them that their dad was working away; he often did that, so they accepted it. They hadn't seen him for a week or so, but he phoned and asked if he could come around for Catherine's fifth birthday at the end of October. Yes of course he could I said. The girls were so pleased to see him and I could see that he was deeply upset, but there was no way back now. He stayed for the afternoon and then the moment I was dreading came. The girls thought he was back from work and staying home with us, but he had to go. They were really upset and I wished I had told them before. I think I said something like "Dad hasn't finished his job yet and he has to go back to work". He left looking like a broken man. The girls were crying and didn't want him to go.

When he left I decided to leave it a while longer before telling them the truth. I figured that the longer he worked away from home, the more the girls would get used to him not being around in the week. They didn't know he was living less than a mile away with his ex-wife and her family. His ex had told him I wasn't to be given a contact number for him. She obviously didn't want her life disrupted like mine and the girls' had been. Anyway, it led to more bad feelings between us. We had been abandoned, or at least that's how it felt. So I had no contact number in case I needed him in an emergency; I heard later that he did what she told him to avoid trouble.

Eventually I had to tell the girls that their dad was living away from home because we couldn't live together any more, and I told them where he was living. Lucy, I think, had worked it out after a few weeks, but she hadn't said anything. It was more difficult to try to explain to Catherine. They were upset, and I felt so sad and guilty.

At one point I thought I should try again with John, but I just couldn't. After a few weeks of seeing him regularly twice a week, they seemed OK again. I think they saw more of him now than they had when we had been together, because he used to go work at six or before and most times came home when they were asleep and he would work most weekends as well. They looked forward to seeing him and he always managed to take them somewhere and buy them dinner. They loved their treats with him. I had no spare money to take them anywhere, so I was glad for them, and it made me feel slightly better.

Sometimes during very bad or cold weather he had started to take them to his ex-wife's home and they used to have something to eat there, I think John got it for them. I wasn't aware of anything wrong until a few years down the road Lucy told me how awful John's ex-wife had been to Catherine – apparently she was OK with Lucy but couldn't stand Catherine. Catherine hadn't said anything at the time but then she was only five. Lucy was eight, almost nine, so she remembered, but I guess it wasn't until she got older that she realised that the way Catherine had been treated wasn't right. It broke my heart to think of all my little girl had been going through, and this was happening just around the corner while I was at home thinking everything was OK. Even writing this down now, all these years later, it still pulls at my heart.

I did ask John about what had happened but he was clueless, he had no idea what I was talking about. I believe that whatever had happened it was done without him knowing. I hated the woman with a passion after that and wanted to go and pull her head off, but I didn't. I believe in karma, so I just waited. In any case, she has been dead for quite a few years now.

Although it was a rough few years, I did have some fun. I had never been to a night club and I didn't drink. Having a baby at 16 and another at 19 with a mum who kept a close eye on me, I never got the chance. So on a Tuesday night back in February 1991, aged 40, I experienced my first nightclub. Yep, I loved it, and the fun went on for about five years on and off at different places. After about a year of doing this and drinking a couple of lagers every time because I didn't know what to drink, someone introduced me to vodka – bad move. But I only used to drink once or twice a week when I went out, for one thing I couldn't afford to and for another it didn't really bother me that much. John used to look after the girls when I had a night out, but he did set a time limit on it – 3 am was as late as I could be to start with and then 2 am and then 1am, so it really wasn't worth going in the end because it took us 45 minutes to get there and the same back.

At that time I met a guy who became pretty helpful in lots of ways. Pete knew a bit about me and how I struggled. I was never in love with him, we just became friends. If I had a day when the girls were with their dad he would take me out somewhere, usually to an old castle or museum– he liked the same kinds of things as me. My nightclub days were over by then, I had got it out of my system and it didn't interest me any more.

There were days when I wouldn't have coped without my friends, and Pete in particular. Sometimes my old car wouldn't start and he would drive 50 miles to come over and sort it out. One year as I was planning to do my annual run down to Devon he asked if he could pop down for a day and meet me at my parents. They knew about him, so it wouldn't be a surprise. The girls and I set off with a full tank of petrol and five pounds. I felt the girls looked as good as I could make them look in their old clothes and hand-me-downs – I didn't want Mum and Dad thinking I couldn't cope. Anything brand new I usually bought out of a catalogue and most of mine came from Oxfam. Good job I was still handy with a sewing machine.

We would arrive at my mum and dads 400-year-old detached thatched cottage, and then I didn't have to worry about money for a whole week. It went like this; they would give me pocket money, yep that's right pocket money, usually about £25 for the week, so that I wouldn't have to ask them for anything. They fed us, took us into town, or to Exeter, and maybe a farm or something. Mum did not do restaurants because of her chronic OCD, something a lot of people didn't realise she had. She had a food phobia and would only eat what she had cooked herself. I asked my auntie about it once, and she said Mum had always been that way, even as a young woman, but it definitely got worse the older she got. If she had no other choice than to eat out, she would order something like fish, even though she never ate it because she thought the bones might choke her. She couldn't have cooked fish any way she had never cooked it in her life as she didn't like the smell of it. Are you beginning to get the drift? Yes, she was a nightmare.

Anyway it gave me a week off cooking, though if I did offer to peel some potatoes she would stand behind me watching. I remember my Nan, who had been a head chef in London, shouting at Mum for not eating what she had cooked for her and saying "you'd think I was trying to bleeding poison you," and Mum would try to eat it and you could see the terror on her face,

Christ knows why she was like that. I know it had an impact on me as a child and growing up as I lived with my parents for years and was with my mum almost every day, so I thought what she did was normal and I didn't know until I was in my forties that you didn't have to cremate everything you cooked so you wouldn't die of food poisoning.

You were hardly allowed to eat anything that was uncooked. She caught me eating a raw mushroom (I had peeled it first), and she screamed at me "Stop, you can't eat that, it's raw!" So as you can see, it was hard work going anywhere with her.

She did cook a lovely Sunday roast though, so tasty, though it took ages to eat because it had the texture of very tough crackling. Mum would always blame the butcher, and she always had a word about the 'tough' meat he gave her last week. I have seen the local butcher, where she went every day, disappear into the freezer and leave one of his colleagues to deal with her. That was my mum. In fact because she went shopping every day to buy what she would call 'fresh food', my dad thought at one time that she was having an affair with the butcher. Christ, the poor butcher used to dread her going in everyday and making a fuss. Not meat from the window, it had to come out of the fridge and then she might have it she might not. I've seen this poor bloke drag an enormous long piece of beef out of his fridge just for her to say "I want a piece cut out of the middle of that, just enough for two people, thank you". So he hacked up this piece of beef, which was probably worth something like £100, just to cut a piece right out of the middle which set my mother back about £2.50.

Anyway, my friend Pete arrived half way through the week and was made welcome by my mum and dad. I think they thought I might marry him and settle down. They had it so wrong. I didn't really know what he was doing there – he had just said he wanted to talk to my parents. We all sat down to tea and biscuits and he began to tell them, to my horror, how I was struggling with money and how hard I worked to keep going. He sang my praises and I sat and listened in silence, thinking this can only end up badly. I had never seen my dad listen to someone without making them feel stupid. Anyway the outcome was that very little happened, except that they now knew how hard I was trying on my own, and Pete said that's what they had needed to know.

They never asked me anything after he left, and after a few days we went home and I dreaded it. Dad did his usual thing and took my car to the petrol garage and filled it up, and then we were off. When we got home someone had tried to break in, and it was only prevented because Pete had put a big bolt on the kitchen door to make it safe the week before. It was little things like that I remember. Like the time my old gas fire packed up and another friend came around and took it out and opened up the chimney so that we could have a fire. Another friend knew I would have nothing to burn on it and brought me a load of wood it was so kind of them. My oldest and best friend, to this day, gave me money to buy the girls Christmas presents because I just didn't have enough. Meanwhile the rest of my family went on their way without ever really knowing.

The house was now going to be repossessed because of mortgage arrears and the council got involved to re-house us. My biggest worry was the upheaval for my girls again, and change of schools. I personally was glad at the thought of getting the hell out of that freezing cold house. So the day came for us to be thrown out. No one was there to help us, although they all knew what was going to happen; I didn't even get a phone call. But Pete was there. He had helped over the past weeks to get me organized and packed. Social Services provided a lorry and two men to help move my furniture, so it didn't cost too much, and with Pete's help we were got out of there.

The council house was meant to be temporary, and it was in an awful part of town. The schools were terrible, which was such a worry. I had fought so hard to keep the girls at good schools and now it was going to be awful for them. Thing is the council, housing association or whoever don't take any of that into consideration. You are made to feel worthless and you're thrown into awful places and put next to people who have no intention of working if they can help it. I used to see a few of them going down to the shops when they had got their giro on Friday morning to stock up on cheap strong lager and fags for the weekend. Now I am a great believer in live and let live, and if someone wants to live that way then best of luck to them. What really used to get me wound up was that I was then 46 and still working hard to avoid having to claim any more benefits than I could help, while some of these people young men and women just sat home all day. I wished I could have sat home all day.

The girls started their schools and Catherine's was OK, but Lucy's was awful. We were there for a year, and then we were told that the council was going to give us a permanent home. When I heard where it was I went mad. The area was well known in the town as the worst place to live. I refused to move there and the council said in that case we would have to be placed in temporary accommodation again. I couldn't bear the thought of all that upheaval again, so after holding out for a few weeks I gave in; they were not going to change their minds. I asked them why they would put us in a place like that and they said they did it because they thought it might rub off on these people and teach them to live a more decent life if they were influenced by people like me, who actually worked for a living.

So that was that again. I had managed to get an old Citroen Dyane, bright yellow and quite old and in immaculate condition, with the help of Jane, who lent me some money. It had been someone's pride and joy and now it was mine. In the flat they had housed us in I had to leave it in the road outside, and because the flat we were in didn't overlook the road I used to be nervous of someone wrecking it. It had a removable hood. One day I went out to get in it and there must have been six kids jumping all over the roof and bonnet. I shouted at them and they got off, but I was afraid of their parents, who were always fighting and screaming at each other. Just six doors away from me someone had set fire to a car and it was completely burnt out.

I approached a woman I knew slightly from the church I went to and asked her if I could put it in her garage for a while until I sorted something more permanent out and she agreed. She gave me a key to her garage and we used to walk down the hill to hers every day and get the car. It solved the problem, for now at least.

We had been there for four months when it got bad. I had been told by different people that when you were housed in this place you were there for good, you never got out.

Lucy was having trouble at school, and it got so bad that one afternoon she was chased by several girls out of the school. They wanted to beat her up, just because her face didn't fit. Lucy was such a good student and a quiet girl, never any bother at school until she had had to go to this one. The one friend she did have ran with her and took her into her house until it was safe for her to get home. They are still the best of friends and very close after all these years, and they are both in their thirties now.

After that I had to watch as my little girl of twelve with the long plait down her back turned into a girl I didn't recognize. She seemed to grow up overnight. Her hair was tied up in a topknot and makeup and short skirts. I hated it. I had always made sure she dressed for her age, not that I had to try, Lucy had never been streetwise and she was so innocent, but this bloody place had ruined her, and I had lost my little girl. She was never any trouble really, it was just the way she looked twelve going on fifteen, and I wasn't too keen on some of the kids she was hanging around with either. So within a few weeks the place had changed her.

Catherine was OK. She was still at middle school, but in two years she would be at Lucy's school too. Lucy had stopped going because she was too frightened. I had spoken to the school several times about the bullying, and they said they couldn't do anything about it unless it was proven. Well I do have a hot temper sometimes, especially when it comes to protecting my own. I said she wouldn't be back until I thought she was going to be safe. So the threats from the school started. I became so angry and almost going crazy knowing she would have to go back.

Then it happened. The flat we lived in was on two levels. We went in on the ground floor where the bedrooms and bathroom were, you went downstairs to the living room and kitchen. One morning I got up and went to the front door to pull the door curtain back and saw that the bottom of the curtain and the carpet were burnt. I saw the matches and bits of wood and paper that someone had pushed through the letterbox during the night. I felt ill. If the fire had started properly we wouldn't have got out, as we had to go past the front door to get downstairs and we wouldn't have been able to. We couldn't have got out of the bedroom windows because they were on the next floor with a long drop to the back garden. We would all have died.

I was shaking uncontrollably; I think it was shock. I didn't wake the girls up but waited until 9 am and phoned the council. I shut myself in my bedroom and went hysterical, sobbing and crying. The woman I spoke to seemed very concerned about what I told her. I had said that I was going to call the police and they needed to get us out of here as soon as possible as our lives were in danger. I had to go to the doctor's for a note to say that he felt we needed to be re-housed. Of course I had to tell him what had happened and I got really upset again. I think he must have thought I was heading for a breakdown, but he did seem indifferent about it all, as if it happened all the time. It made me feel like an idiot. He did write the letter though and it was pretty good.

I had to move well away from this town and start again. Lucy and Catherine never went back to school and within five months of going into that hellhole we were out of it, 25 miles away in a new town, Hemel Hempstead. We were given another ground floor flat, which was good because it meant that our two cats could come with us. Lucy started going to a church school that had a good reputation and she never looked back. She didn't make any lasting friends there though, she still kept in touch with her best friend back home, and she used to go back to Wycombe whenever she could to be with her best friend.

I got a job working in a residential care home and I really enjoyed it. It was about six miles away in another town. I used to work Saturday and Sundays 7am till 4pm, so that helped cut down my benefits quite a bit, and I was still looking for other work that would fit around the girls' school. I worked in the care home for four years, every weekend and one night duty on Wednesday, which meant I could go there and sleep the night, but I was there in case the other career needed help during the night. John had the girls each weekend, either at his or at mine –by then he had moved away from Wycombe to be nearer the girls and also to help me go to work and not have to ask him for anything, so it worked both ways I guess.

CHAPTER 11

A bolt from the blue

After about a year of working at the care home, the
opportunity of a job in the local hospital came along. I
went for an interview and got it. It involved working
in the pathology department in haematology, and I
loved it there and wasn't surrounded by lots of others,
which suited me. It took me a while to get used to it as
there was so much to learn, but after a few months I
became good at it and wished I had done something
like this years ago. I worked Monday to Friday 9am
till 3.30pm. The hospital were very understanding
about my situation, being a single mum with no
support and new to the town, so they let me go half an

hour before my shift should have ended to get the girls, who were at different schools and finished at different times.

Because my income had improved I was able to come right off benefits at last. It's such a good feeling to be totally independent. We had enough to pay the rent and all the bills – there wasn't much left for luxuries, but we managed OK. I even had enough to run my car properly, without which I would never have got these two jobs. But I was working seven days a week and one night shift and I was constantly tired. When I got home at 7.30 Wednesday morning after doing my night shift at the care home, John was raring to go, and I had to quickly get changed, freshen up, get the girls' breakfast and make sure they were ready by 8.15 to get them to school. I had been doing my two jobs for three years now and I knew I wouldn't be able to keep them both going for much longer, but the thought of my income dropping again kept me going.

Then one Sunday lunchtime I was working at the care home and doing a bit of washing up when I noticed that I couldn't feel the hot water, and my hand felt slightly numb. I was a bit concerned after what had happened to me 14 years earlier. I told Margaret, the care home owner, who always came in on Sundays to cook the meals for the residents, and she couldn't understand it. I thought she might have some idea what was wrong as she was a nurse. She said I should get it checked out, so I went to the doctor's the next day. The doctor referred me to a neurologist in the hospital where I worked, and I got to see him quickly – you do tend to jump the queue when you're an NHS employee. He sent me for an MRI scan (Pete took me – good old Pete, he was always there if I needed him). I waited for a month or so and then my GP asked me to come in and see her about the results. She looked kind of worried when I went into the surgery. She had a letter in her hands and she asked me to sit down. I just remember thinking, please god let me be OK, my girls still need me.

Anyway the outcome of the scan was that I had multiple sclerosis. I felt my stomach jump. I had worked for a man with MS and had watched the deterioration in him over two years from walking unaided to walking with a stick to not walking at all. I asked her twice if it really was MS. I couldn't believe it.

I had to go home and think about it and try and work out what I was going to do. The first person I told was Pete, and he was shocked. The thing is with MS that people who have it always look so well; I didn't look ill, let alone terminal.

I had to go and see my neurologist again; he was so nice to me. He told me that all MS cases are different. There were four types, which I didn't know until then.

He said mine was benign so it shouldn't progress too soon. I asked him if the numbness I had felt all those years ago when they took me into hospital and couldn't find anything wrong with me was MS and he said yes. But they can't diagnose it until you have had two episodes, which I now had, and then they could give me a diagnosis. He asked if I had pain and I did, quite badly in my left arm, so he gave me medication, and that stopped the pain within a couple of days, so still I take it now and again to control the pain.

What you can't control is the strange feelings you get. I quite often have the sensation of someone throwing ice cold water over me, usually on my hand, arm or head. It makes me jump out of my skin and then I sit there trying to dry this invisible water off myself. Another thing that hasn't really gone away is the numbness, but it comes and goes and it's patchy, just the odd bits on my body go numb. I also sometimes can't feel heat, so I have to be careful around hot pans. I remember once holding onto a radiator that I thought was cold and it wasn't until I got a throbbing pain in my hand and realized it was red hot. Also cold can feel hot. In a nutshell, if someone asks me about it and how it makes me feel I say to them "I'm light sensitive, heat sensitive and touch sensitive, so turn the lights off, turn the fans on and don't touch me!" That will normally break the ice if people don't know how to be around me.

You just have to laugh at it and realise that worse things happen. I have lived with MS now for over thirty years, and although I have my bad days, on the whole I'm pretty well. I find that as long as I pace myself I can function, and if I overdo it I don't function, you just learn to adapt. The only thing that infuriates me is the people who look down their noses at me when I pull into a disabled car park space. I have had people approach me and get right up to my face and ask if I realise this is a disabled space as I'm fumbling to get my blue badge out and shove it in their face. I've got so used to it over the years I just tell them "I'm sorry I'm laughing with my friend", or "I'm sorry I don't fit your idea of someone who is disabled, or that I don't walk with a limp and I have no lump on my back, because you know what? You shouldn't be laughing and you should have a limp or a lump or both, because YOU are a disabled. Fuck you all!" You can be sure they don't approach me again, the self-righteous bastards.

My neurologist asked me how my parents were about the whole MS thing and I said they hadn't talked about it with me, although I had tried to talk to them. He said it was normal for parents to be like that around MS because we all look so bloody well most of the time and there are no visible signs that we are ill, unless we get into a wheelchair. He did warn me that I would find this with most people it was a kind of ignorance. They don't understand it, and unless they knew about it they won't get it.

When I first told Jane she asked what it was, and Louise went and read up on it. I left the leaflets I was given to read lying around for my parents to look at, but they never did. They had moved back from Devon to be nearer to the family as Dad was in poor health and they needed a bit more support. Mum would still expect me to take her shopping twice a week, even if I was having a relapse of extreme fatigue. I think she thought I was just lazy.

My work was beginning to suffer, and on the advice of the neurologist I gave up working in the care home. He said that stress and overwork would more than likely bring on another relapse. I still had my work in the hospital and they were so good to me, they even said they would get me a chair on wheels so that I didn't have to keep getting up and down all the time. If I went missing for more than twenty minutes they would send out a search party to find me and check that I was OK. At least these people understood what was going on, and I felt so well looked after.

Louise had gone to live in Australia some years before and I missed her and the kids so much sometimes. She used to write to me quite often, and she always sent me and her sisters gifts. They were all coming back home for Christmas 1999 and going back in the New Year. She asked me if I would like to go back with them for a holiday with the view to maybe moving out there for good. I was so happy. I remember having bronchitis that year and being in bed for most of it. But it was so good to have her back and to be going back with them was fantastic.

I told my mum – and she hit the roof. She said I couldn't just walk away like that. I said I wasn't going to, that I would be back and I would want the girls to go with me, and if they wouldn't then I wouldn't go. She really had the hump with me, so I asked her round for a chat. She said she thought I was being selfish and asked how she would manage. I told her to ask Jane to help her out for a few weeks. I also took her into my kitchen and opened my fridge and asked her what she could see in it. She looked and said, "milk and bread". "That's right I said, milk and bread, so don't talk to me about being selfish. I have to take you shopping twice a week and stand watching you fill you trolley up with loads of food I know won't get eaten, and I'm standing behind you with a loaf of bread and some sugar and you never once ask me if I need any food for the girls."

I hate talking about her like this, but Christ she was so greedy with money and everything else. Her favourite saying when we got home and she was unpacking £80 worth of groceries (and that was just the weekend's shopping) was "I'm all right Jack". I used to want to push her inside the fridge with the bloody food. I told her I might have a chance at a better life in Australia and that Louise was going to sponsor me. Well, it went from bad to worse.

So off I went to Australia, and I was there for about five weeks. The hospital were very good about it and said to take my time and stay as long as I wanted. Then after five weeks of fantastic weather and spending time with my grandchildren and daughter, I had to come home to get back to work. Freezing cold February after 34 degrees in Australia was awful. When I got back I knew that I wouldn't be going to Australia as it was too late to move the girls, they were settled.

Life went on, and after some time I had to reduce the hours I worked as I was in pain and suffering fatigue again, so I was down to four hours every morning. They told me that as long as I could manage four hours a day I would keep my job, but if it was any less they would have to let me go. I managed for another 18 months and then couldn't do any more.

My neurologist asked to see me and said he thought it was time I took early retirement. I was 51 and didn't feel ready, but I wasn't functioning on a daily basis and I didn't know how I would feel from one day to the next. He advised me to apply for disability living allowance, and after a few months I got it. What a relief, I wouldn't have to worry any more about money. My rent was paid and my council tax was paid – they had been the two biggest worries. We had enough for food as well, for once. It made me realise why some people claim benefits – when they get so much help, why they should work? I had worked all my life and for long hours and still struggled. But I wouldn't change that.

My friends at the hospital gave me a lovely silver necklace and matching earrings and a big bunch of flowers and a very large card which everyone had signed. They said it had been the most they had ever collected for anyone. As I said, it was the one place I had really been understood. I was going to miss it, and I knew that if it hadn't been for MS I would still be there. I got a small NHS pension, not much as I had only been there four and a half years, but it helps.

In 2002 I had the chance to move out of the town and into the country via an exchange, and I took it. I have now been here for 15 years, the longest I've stayed anywhere. I live quite a lonely life, never having found anyone to share it with, but I have an amazing family all around me, all grown up now of course, eight grandchildren and number nine on the way and five great grandchildren, and I am the happiest I've ever been. My MS is stable and I can still get around in my car, and I say thank you every day for that.

My dad passed away in 2005 aged 80 after being bedridden for three years. I went to see him on the day he died and held his hand, but he pulled it away. It confused and upset me, but didn't really surprise me; he obviously didn't want me there. I went home. Three hours later Jane came to my door to tell me he had passed away. I went back to Mum's. She seemed OK, upset of course but not what I expected. She seemed calm. Maybe it was a relief after all those years of caring for him, and he wasn't an easy man, he still managed to control her from his bed.

My relationship with my dad had deteriorated over the last ten years or so, I never knew why. I think he was disappointed in me. I remember going into see him a couple of times a week and he always smiled when I walked in, until he saw that it wasn't Jane. He loved her unconditionally and she could do no wrong in his eyes. The older he got, the more distance came between us. It didn't really upset me as I was used to it; it had been that way from the day she was born. I really didn't want to go and see him every week, but Mum made it hard for me as I had to go around to hers twice a week to take her shopping and she would say "go and see your father". So I would trip up the stairs, dreading it. Would he be pleased to see me or would he just ignore me? Or would he shake his fist at me? I was still afraid, even though he was old and in a bed he couldn't get out of.

When he passed away I was relieved for my mum and myself and also for him. He had been a very proud man and to see him that way in bed was awful, having to have everything done for him. He had lost his hearing and was losing his eyesight, so in his last year he couldn't read a paper or watch TV, and he just lay there fossilized. He couldn't even smoke any more because it made him ill. I know this sounds terrible, but the first thing that came into my mind when I heard he had passed away was, "Thank god I won't have to see him any more".

I have to hang onto the good memories of him I have. In his way he had been a good father, and I knew that when the going got tough my dad got tougher. He would never have let anyone harm me, I know that, but I just wish I could have got closer to him; I would have loved a cuddle from him, my protector.

After he died I wanted to take my mum away on holiday with me; she had only flown once, a few years before, so I got her a new passport. I had plans that we could travel together. I would take her all over the world with me and she would love it. At last I had my mum all to myself. I was going to make up for all those years when she had looked after everyone else and no one seemed to have appreciated her. Of course, in reality Mum would never have been able to do this, with her chronic OCD and fear of food, but it was a wonderful dream while it lasted.

Mum passed away in 2007 aged 77 at home, in her own bed of lung cancer, 17 months after my dad. I sat on her bed and held her hand and told her that I loved her, and then, peacefully, she left me. She had been told that she didn't have long to live so I went and stayed with her, and she only lived two months after her diagnosis. During that short time we had together, she was different. She told me things I hadn't known about. We talked about her life as a child and about her mum and dad. She showed me things that had been kept out of the way that I never knew existed. She told me she was doing this so that I would remember it.

After my mum left I cried every day for three years. I couldn't seem to accept it. I even went back to places where she had lived, looking for her. I thought I was going crazy, but apparently it sometimes happens to people after they have lost someone close to them – it's called searching behaviour. I knew I wouldn't find her, but I kept looking.

A month after Mum died, Catherine moved out to be with her boyfriend and travel around Australia for two years. After all the years of bringing up children and having such a busy life I didn't know what to do with myself. I did have Sally, my little poodle, but she died five months later. I was grief stricken, and so lonely. It's taken a while for me to get back to just me and getting to know myself again. From the age of just sixteen all I had known was bringing up my children. They were my life, but now I realised I had to get on without them and begin to make a life for myself.

This book has been a kind of cleansing for me. It's taken me years to write it, with the guilt I felt when talking about my dad. I can't count the number of times since I started it that I've deleted parts or changed it in some way. But a year ago I decided to just tell it as it was. It may upset some members of the family, but this is my story, not theirs.

As for Mum, I miss her every day, but I don't go looking for her any more. Her life had been full and my brother and I had been very much part of it, with her crazy ways and all that came with it, and despite everything, I knew without a doubt that she had loved us completely.